Mr.

Marcelino Huranga-

I hope you enjoy reading
this book as much as
enjoyed writing it

thank you

E Sauvedi

MW00592748

Jersey, My Love

Exileine Jean Michel Samedi

NEWMAN SPRINGS PUBLISHING
320 Broad Street
Red Bank, NJ 07701

First originally published by Newman Springs Publishing 2023

ISBN 978-1-68498-086-4 (Hardcover)
ISBN 978-1-68498-087-1 (Digital)

Printed in the United States of America

To
the Jerseymen
who cherish
the precious Garden State

To
immigrants
from everywhere and elsewhere
seeking to realize
the great American Dream

With
respect, dignity, and gratitude

Everything God does, he does it right. No need for palette or tablet to engineer a perfect job. He just does it! I think New Jersey is his favorite place to have pampered it with such special touch. It seems that some parts of the Garden State, the great Creator designed them with his bare hands and personally hung them from the sky.

Acknowledgments

To my husband, my children, and grandchildren, you have supported me as I continue to grow as an author.
Also, a special thank-you to JCW.

Jersey, My Love!

A man who escaped death in Haiti ends up in New Jersey in search of peace. But trying to breathe and leave the past behind is just blurry and distractive perception. New events bring him back to the same nightmares of torturing and horrifying moments. Only this time, he looks more like a suspect than a victim.

To get out of this deep hole of desperation is not easy. But when love is complicit with the goodness of nature, miracles happen.

Jersey, My Love! is written for people that are trying to find the balance between fear and hope, love and enterprise, those struggling with transitions and trying to grow roots, and for those who dream the American dream.

Jersey, My Love! is an advocacy for the youth and a call to the New Jersians who have yet to discover how marvelous and beautiful their state is!

No matter how clear seems to be the horizon
Obstacle often comes from opposite direction
But whatever the challenge you must face
Don't let anxiety and fear rob your peace

My Love!

With infinite gratitude, I say it
Aloud and with joy, I cry it
Like a branch by the storm devastated
Slaughtered and its trunk detached
I was jostled by impetuous winds
Going adrift according to the floods
You took my hand and showed me the way
You placed in my heart hope for another day
With kindness, you have soothed the fear
You restored the dream and dried the tears
Facing and overcoming difficulties
But always thankful for opportunities
This frail branch is finally rooted in the Garden
Bringing new flowers to your precious Eden
I am here; I feel well; I am okay
In your arms, I want to stay
Forget my origin? I will never
Jersey my love! In my heart you will be forever

Jersey, My Love!

Premiere Partie
New York / New Jersey

Hope for the best
Be aware of the worst
Struggle without giving up
Life and hope will lift you up

-1-

Jersey City, City of My Childhood, I Am Coming Back to You

It is four thirty in the afternoon; New York City is in chaos! People on foot—we don't know where they have come from or where they are going—form a real human tide, filling the streets to the brim. In a terrible traffic jam, private cars, taxis, and buses stop bumper to bumper every minute, obstructing the way to ambulances, firefighters, and police cars who, no matter what, want without delay to arrive at emergency points. Seeking to break through the traffic, the drivers of these vehicles deemed priority do not care much about the endless sirens that push the rest of the population to the brink of insanity. It is not exaggeration to say, at peak times, hell is in transit on earth.

At the Port Authority subway station, the tension is no less high. The inbound and outbound transports, already overdue, are crossed by hundreds in a hubbub of smoke and horn. The facility is so huge that it is considered a city itself.

This place is a junction point, a melting pot, or a babel, where travelers coming from different sectors of the state or even from different parts of the world would cross, bumping to each other and speaking all kinds of languages. Like ants on summer days, they are moving incessantly, running in different directions and dragging their baggage before departing to their respective destinations.

Always in activity, trains and buses never stop; taxis are carrying passengers in and out day and night. After all, *New York never sleeps.*

At the gates, the lines get longer and longer. Some first timers are checking their schedule and their watches every couple of minutes. Too nervous to be patient, they are pacing in the waiting areas like tigers in cages. Some others who are too tired to stand on the line would sit on their luggage with their half-closed eyes, thinking only God knows what. But to others lost in long conversations with their cell phones glued to their ears, it seems time does not exist.

Anyway, everyone is carrying their own burden, dealing with their own trouble. Everyone is looking forward to getting their way. You must take care of yourself and not mind another people's business.

This station seems to be a maze. If you happen to take a tour just for the great pleasure of visiting, you will not stop going in circle running the chance to get lost. Now it remains to be seen if your feet will respond to the adventure. But thank goodness for technology. The signs and directions displayed at every staircase make it easy to find the way out.

It was the end of January; the winter was beating in full swing over New York City. The citizens who did not have an urgent need to be outside tried to keep warm behind their closed doors while observing through the windows the vestiges of the last storm. The tenacious snow that had been piled up on the ground for more than a week was turning to a disgusting dark mud instead of melting away.

At Port Authority, the bad weather was not any match for regular activities. The gates were crowded as usual; people covered with layers over layers were as always ready, willing, and able. Business is business; it neither waits nor gets intimidated by the winter: Business is money!

Around 1:30 p.m. that day, the activities were at their peak. A slim man, tall and in his late twenties with a shopping bag slung over his shoulder, was going from station to station, looking for his transport network without paying much attention to the signs. Dragging on his left leg, he had a look of despair and extreme loneliness on his face. The long-sleeve sweater, blue jeans, and sneakers, a bit too big for his feet, were not enough to protect him from the brutal cold: he was shaking. Just looking at him, you could tell that life had not been easy. Although people were busy, taking care of business, they could not help turning around, observing him. This man had come a long way, or to be more precise, it seemed that he had escaped from hell. He asked for information; but his hoarse voice, like he had cried too much, joined to his heavy accent was a handicap.

From the ground floor, he walked his way up. He continued by the food court with the same restlessness, but the smell of all those ethnic foods stopped him in his tracks. The delicious aroma of the frying onion, pepper, and garlic hit him right in his empty stomach.

This aroma reminds me of Marie Marthe's pate kode, he thought. *My God, I can't believe she is gone. There will never be any better cordon bleu than she made.*

To buy something, he pulled out of his pocket a rusty and dirty old wallet and wandered around for a minute. The diversity of the dishes looked so attractive—from the Subway sandwiches to the paneer kadai, a popular Indian dish; the falafel, a famous Egyptian sandwich; and the Cuban café espresso. He had a variety of choices; but the stress, the worry, and a terrible anguish consuming him took away his appetite.

He finally got to gate 225G on the fourth floor. There, the line was even longer but a bit quieter. These people already knew the routine for going back and forth every day. Instead of driving to work in the morning, their best bet was public transportation: time is money. Most of them were executives or office managers working around New York and Philadelphia. Still dressed in their suits and ties, they were waiting patiently for the New Jersey Transit buses, but the look in their sleepy eyes claimed that enough was enough. Even their briefcases seemed too heavy to handle. In fact, there was nothing new; at Port Authority, the days are always too long.

A New Jersey-bound bus had just turned into the station. The line rushed in, and in less than two minutes, the bus was crowded. The driver was about to leave when a man came speeding on his legs like he was running away from something.

Waving his hat, he yelled, "Stop, please. Stop!" before jumping in.

Right away, he pulled a five-dollar bill out of his pocket, asking if anybody had change. Since no one paid attention, he put the bill in and hung on to the rail in silence. This man was the same one who had been looking for his way since the subway stations. He finally made it onto the bus headed toward New Jersey.

Since it is located right next to New York, people commuting between these two states do not have any problems. You just jump on the interstate bus or hop on the Path train, and you are right there. The 99S is amazingly fast. From Port Authority, it usually crosses the Lincoln Tunnel; and in minutes, you are in New Jersey. Via Kennedy Boulevard, it runs through Hoboken, West New York, Union City, Jersey City, and all the way to Bayonne. Sitting on this bus, you can get a good glimpse of Hudson County, so dear to New Jersey.

As the bus was running, people were getting off along the way. The man, now sitting on a comfortable seat, did not stop looking around. The streets, the houses, the people walking by with their heavy coats on, and the businesses—all seemed so strange. He was astonished; everything looked so different. Leaning back on his seat, he closed his tired eyes for a minute. Meanwhile, his mind was flying and flying, and only he knew how far it got. As he tried to relax, he took a deep breath. Instead, a mixed feeling of regret and melancholy invaded him, and his stressed-out mood soon changed to sadness. Suddenly he pressed his stomach with both hands.

"Merde!" he whispered, and teardrops rolled over his face.

Sitting across the aisle, a middle-aged woman who was observing all that time finally addressed him before leaving the bus.

"My son, what happened? Where are you going?"

Believe it or not, he responded, "I am going to get a hug from my mother. I am looking for a bit of rest."

"That is so nice of you," said the lady with sad admiration. "I have a son about your age, and I would be overjoyed if he were to come and visit me for just a hug."

The lady got off, wondering. *What kind of tragedy is running this poor man heart? What kind of hell is burning behind this handsome and mysterious physiognomy? God willing, he finds the rest that he needs. But as soon as I get home, I am going call my son, John, and ask him why he doesn't come and visit me for just a hug.*

The bus was going and going; the man, completely exhausted from the ups and downs of the day, finally rested his head and snoozed off.

"Hey, you!" yelled the driver as the bus got to Bayonne. "You need to get out."

"What happened?"

"Last stop. You must leave."

"Where are we?"

"Do you know where you are going exactly?"

The conversation could not go too far because of miscommunication. The man finally pulled a piece of paper out of his pocket and handed it to the driver.

"You are going to Jersey City," said the driver, shaking his head in impatience. "I will take you on my way back, but you need to keep your eyes open."

"Okay," he whispered with a deep breath of relief. *Jersey City, city of my childhood, I am coming back to you.*

Jersey City is in the northern part of New Jersey. Between Bayonne to the south and Union City, North Bergen, West New York, and Hoboken to the North, it stretches the heart of the Hudson County like a T-shirt.

It is the hometown of Lady Liberty—a milestone, an icon of greatness, and an omnipresent symbol of freedom and democracy. For years, New York City has been courting her, maintaining, supporting, and claiming her as his. Nevertheless, she remains faithful to New Jersey. We must admit that she is somehow capricious but not frivolous. Just looking at her, you notice that she always has her back turned on the Garden State; but she never moved one step away from the banks of Jersey City. For years and years, Lady Liberty, the great gatekeeper of the United States, has been standing tall and strong at the famous park that carries her name, holding in her left hand a tablet which is an open letter to the world: "Give me your tired, your poor, your huddled masses yearning to breathe free, the wretched refuse of your teeming shore. Send these, the homeless, tempest-tossed to me. I lift my lamp beside the golden door!"

She has been welcoming people from all over the world, brandishing high and tight the torch of liberty as if she is forever proclaiming that the United States of America is a country of freedom. The suffocating chains of oppression had fallen long ago. Now, make no mistake. Call her surrogate or fairy godmother to all if you want, but she is strict. She is just. She plays by the rules. Whoever you are, you need to do it right and with honesty. Like the sun rises to warm up everyone, the flame of liberty is here to enlighten everyone. Just abide by the laws of the land, and you will breathe free.

Facing the mouth of New York Harbor, with her green copper dress symbolizing hope and trust, she never stops inspiring the beautiful Garden State to go greener and greener or demands the sons and daughters of America to cherish and venerate their land from sea to shining sea.

Lady Liberty never departed from her first love, the Garden State, where she has grown deep roots. Nevertheless, her heart belongs to the whole country: the United States of America, which she represents so well. She deserves not only her first name but full recognition from the land.

Jersey City is the second largest city in the state. Besides the main streets such as Route 440, West Side, Bergen, Ocean Avenue, Martin Luther King Drive, Garfield Avenue, etc., one of the most important arteries is the endless Kennedy Boulevard that crosses through five cities altogether; this is the route of the 99S bus, where the poor man was still sitting, waiting on the driver's good faith to make a miraculous stop for him because, at that point in time, he was more lost than footprints on the sand.

The evening had settled over. Most of the businesses were already closed for the day. The forecast had announced a new snowstorm coming. The active population got off work and headed straight to the stores before returning home. With less traffic, the 99S was running faster. It finally crossed Communipaw Avenue and stopped at the corner of Harrison and Kennedy Boulevard.

"Let's go!" yelled the driver

"What?" said the man, jumping off his seat.

"This is your stop. Just walk one more block. Read the sign, and you will see Gifford Avenue."

"Thank you," he replied with a smile that was not too convincing.

The truth, he was more worried than happy. For it was already dark, and it was getting colder. After the ordeal of the day, walking alone in the streets without knowing exactly which door to knock at was not too pleasant.

The man had time to walk half a block when two people who were standing at the corner of Gifford Avenue started walking in his direction with an inquisitive gaze. Suddenly they started running toward him, waving their arms with excitement.

"Hyppolite? Is that you? Over here! Popo, we are here!"

Running toward each other from a different block, the three men finally met at the corner of Jewett Avenue and Kennedy Boulevard, jumping and hugging each other. One of them did not want to let go.

Still hugging Hyppolite, he turned his head toward the sky with tears rolling down his face. *Oh my God! I cannot believe I am looking at my brother again. Thank you. Thank you, dear Lord. If he is still breathing, if his heart is still beating, it is thanks to you. Oh, Lord. Blessed be your name!*

Meanwhile, the other man did not take his fingers off his cell phone. One by one, he called everyone who was out there watching out at a different intersection, just in case Hyppolite took a different route to Gifford Avenue.

"Eh, man, I am at the corner of Kennedy Boulevard and Jewett Avenue. We got him. Where are you?"

"Hello. We are at the corner of Gifford Avenue and West Side Avenue. Do not move. I will be right there."

"Hello. I am at Bergen Avenue and Harrison Street. We are coming."

"Hello. We are at Monticello and Brinkerhoff. Wait for us!"

The last phone call was directed to Méralie, the mother of Hyppolite who, with anxious heart, was waiting at home with two scarves mooring her belt.

"Hello, Mommy. Be happy. We found Popo. Your son is here. We are coming home."

Soon a cortege of eight men and women escorted Hyppolite in an effervescence of joy to the curiosity of the people passing by, who did not understand what was going on.

-2-

The Family

Méralie came the first time to the United States thirty years ago with an American missionary group that was visiting Haiti. At that time, her late mother was reluctant to let her go.

A young woman going to a foreign country with a bunch of strangers, she thought, *wasn't any guaranty for safety.*

She was smart, intelligent, and about to terminate her secondary studies with ambitious plans. But it was not easy; in a family where there is no father around to provide support, neither a powerful godfather who would facilitate a good job, plans are only beautiful dreams that cannot be achieved. She ran the risk of ending up like many of the other girls in the neighborhood: a widow or an abandoned woman struggling tooth and nail to put food on the table for half a dozen children, a living existence where complaining about pain and misery become redundant.

Méralie was well adapted to her family and rooted to their customs, but when it comes to resignation, she was as stubborn as a mule. She was the kind of person who does not give up on a dream or lose hope without a fight. No one must accept poverty as a definite condition of existence. Things are tough, but there had to be a way through. Despite the warning of the family, her character and self-determination boosted her emotional and spiritual immunity; she found strength to rise above fear and doubt.

He who dares nothing wins nothing, she thought.

After days of reasoning, she finally convinced her mother to let her go.

Hoping for a brighter future, she jumped on the opportunity and left Haiti with the missionaries. She took the lead. If she excelled in the right direction, she would pave the way for the ones left behind.

With the help of a Baptist congregation, Méralie settled down in Jersey City. It did not take her long to learn English and land a job at the Jersey City courthouse, where she joined the cleaning crew. After three years, she went back to Haiti, married her high school sweetheart, and returned with him to the US. From this marriage were born four children: Tertulien, Esaie, Hyppolite, and Anne Marie. Hyppolite, also called Popo, was Méralie's favorite child. He was sent to Haiti at six years old to be educated by his paternal grandmother, with whom he had spent a major part of his life. When he was younger, he used to come to US for the summer but just to spend one month with the family. After high school, he studied business administration, opened his own business, and decided to settle on the island for good.

Their father, Jean Philippe, passed away twenty-five years ago from a heart attack. Since then, the family had lived in an apartment building on Gifford Avenue. This building is from one of the multiple affordable housing programs going on, which are a blessing for many families in Jersey City.

Méralie is now sixty-eight years old. Although she was gray haired, she looked quite healthy and young for her age. She was one of those people who religiously follow doctors' recommendations and watch cautiously their diet. Once retired from the court, she embraced the church activities as a new job. Unless she was sick, she never missed her Sunday services or the weekly gathering for Bible studies and prayer meetings.

She had been living in the neighborhood for a long time; she was well-known and respected. But she had a special characteristic that made her children worried sick. They did not know if to consider it as a virtue or interfering in others' business. The fact is that she could not help volunteering herself and counseling people for anything that seemed wrong. Calm and serene with a benevolent look, she was always ready to advocate for someone or give advice to the youngsters. Since she had worked a long time at the courthouse, overhearing lawyers' conversations in the hallways made her feel that she had mastered the art of law.

Although she was strict with her own children, she had a special thought for some adolescents in the neighborhood—these restless teenagers and young adults who were running around, counting on their youth and their energy as if they were invincible. To her, they were just children who were living confused, betrayed, and angry yet still yearning for the love of a family. If they had someone who cared or at least someone to talk to, their life would take another direction.

When the group reached Méralie's front step with Hyppolite, the door was already wide open. It was a very impressive and solemn moment; a mixed feeling of joy and sadness and excitement and repression filled the room. Everybody was happy for the safe return of Hyppolite. They wanted to shout and give thanks, for his life was spared. But at the same time, they were asking, Why that earthquake? Why Haiti? Why so much death and devastation? Why so much suffering?

Standing there with bated breath and her heart racing in her throat, Méralie did not utter a word. Trembling, she looked at Hyppolite and hesitated for a moment as if she did not believe her eyes. Soon her anxious mood gradually faded away to reveal a smile that lit up her face. She could not do anything else but jump into his arms.

Tertulien finally got Hyppolite to refresh and put on the new clothes that had been readied for him. Esaie was sitting in the living room with Yanique, his inseparable other half, his fiancée. The family really appreciated her because, since Esaie met her, he quit his running around with a different girl every day. According to Méralie, God had put this angel in her son's path to rescue him from debauchery and perdition.

Yanique was born in the USA and had just graduated from Christ Hospital Nursing School. Since she had a taste for Haitian music, she took advantage of that special occasion to demonstrate her DJ talent. From the living room, she was managing the sound, blasting a compas Creole that pressured everyone to shake their bodies. The music was playing. People were talking to each other, making comments and asking questions, but Hyppolite did not say much. He was so reserved about the tragedy it was like he wanted to block out the painful memory.

Méralie finally started to get back to herself. As a tear ran down to her face, she brought down the sound and asked everyone to be quiet for a while.

With an explosion of emotions and her hands lifted, she shouted, "Gloire á Dieu!" Blessed be the Lord! She then turned to address the friends and family reunited, "There is a great deal to say this evening, but the emotion is so high that I feel really hesitant to speak out. You see, there is nothing more comforting than hope. After the unfortunate event of January 10 that had shaken the whole world to the core, I did not think anybody in this house would have enough strength to get back to himself. It was too much of a strain to keep composure, but I have been telling you all along to have faith, that God is good. Since the beginning, I was confident that the fresh breeze of a miracle was coming our way.

"I thank you for bringing my son home to me. I thank all of you for being here in this moment so important to the family. There is plenty of food and drink to enjoy. But before we do anything, let us join hands and give thanks to the Lord in prayer."

Everybody held hands together, but since Méralie did not want to let go of her son, they formed a circle around them.

It was Friday evening. Joseph, Tertulien's son, who was supposed to be with his father every weekend, was in the house. As soon as the prayer was over, he approached his father and asked for money to go out with his friends. As the father refused and told him to stay with the family, he got upset.

"I do not know why all this nonsense," he murmured. "Somebody just came from overseas. He did not bring anything of value, and they are welcoming him *comme un roi*. I mean, the man is a nice guy. He is my uncle, but receiving him with such pomp and ceremony, you would think he is the Prodigal Son."

"Joseph, we have guests here," said Tertulien. "Please shut your mouth. You will stay here with everybody, and that is it."

By 9:15 p.m., Anne Marie came in from school with her boyfriend, Mohammad. He was a handsome twenty-five-year-old young man but not very well seen by Méralie. The way he carried himself while speaking with his fingers sticking out did not please her. His long dreaded hair and baggy pants falling down his hips was another shock that clashed with the approval of the whole family. They did not see this relationship with good eyes; they claimed that they did not know anything about this man and his family. According to him, he was self-employed, working in the delivery business, but they were never able to verify that. They were worried about Anne Marie, who was doing everything she could to succeed in life. During the day, she worked a part-time job at Chili's; and in the evening, she studied community services and criminal justice at Hudson County Community College.

She was a loving and caring young lady, always ready to listen and help her people the way she could. But when it came to this man, she kept everybody at a distance. Stubbornly sticking to her opinions regardless of whether she was right or wrong, she was not open to any advice. The family was not at peace; they were just giving her space to open her eyes and get her senses back.

The couple was on their way into the living room where everybody gathered when Joseph jumped right in front of them.

"Auntie Anne, please, I want some money. I got to get something now. My father has not given me my allowance yet. He keeps on telling me to wait. As soon as I get it from him, I will pay you back."

"What is the matter with you?" Anne Marie replied. "Where are you going at this time? There is lot of food here. What is the big emergency? Your uncle just came home. Don't you think, in a moment like this, you should stick together with the family? Whatever you need out there, you will get it tomorrow."

"Please, please, Auntie, do me this favor."

"I saw two of your friends outside. Are they waiting for you? Didn't people tell you not to get acquainted with those boys?"

"I was only speaking to Edmond, who lives down the block. He just arrived from Barbados last week."

Mohammad, in a spontaneous and frustrating reaction, reached down into his pocket and handed a twenty-dollar bill to Joseph, who immediately exited the door.

"He is only fourteen years old. He is just a kid without any experience in life," said Anne Marie, upset. "You are spoiling him. What you just did is wrong. I do not want him to pick up bad manners. At this age, kids have tendency to listen more to friends than their parents. His father just said no! Giving him money is an encouragement to disobedience and rebellion."

"Is it prejudice? Why are you talking about his friends? What is wrong with those boys? I wish I had a father around to provide for me when I was his age," said Mohammad.

"I do not have anything against these kids, but some of them drink, smoke, and God knows what else. They take pleasure hurting themselves. They are flirting with pain, if not death. This is not the example I want for my nephew."

Joseph lived in Paterson with his mother. She had custody of the boy, who usually spent the weekends in Jersey City. The situation became very problematic because being raised in two different environments was just conflictual. The father was strict; he imposed discipline and wanted the boy to attend church every Sunday. The mother, as a young woman living in a new relationship with two other children, was more open; she had a different concept of life.

Tertulien got married two years ago. His wife was still in Haiti waiting on the immigration office to approve her residence application. Meanwhile, he was the right hand of his mother. Always in control, he was the one running errands for the house. He stayed in contact with the doctor, checked Méralie's medications, and kept everything in order. He was sitting in the living room, giving explicit details to his sister on how they picked up Hyppolite and brought him home, when they heard an unpleasant voice in the hallway. It was a neighbor coming their way, angry as hell. Since the door was already wide open, he just went in.

"You people! Do you have a hearing problem? Why so much noise? Don't you know what time it is?"

"You are right, sir, and I am sorry," said Esaie, turning the radio down. "It was not our intention to disturb our neighbors. If you do not mind, come and sit with us for just a moment while I speak to you. It is true the Haitians are loud, but they are good and humble people. In the worst moment of our life, even crying, we always have a song on our lips. In the bad times, we bend together in solidarity. When the relief comes, we celebrate. We raise our glasses high even if we have to toast with water. We are excited this evening because my brother is alive. Everybody thought that he perished in the earthquake that ravaged our people back home. Today, with great emotion, we finally got him back, and that is the reason for so much exuberance. Please have a drink with us. I know this should be good news for you too."

As a real peacemaker, Esaie got the neighbor to calm down and finally convinced him to stay with them. Not only did he join the party, but he was the last guest to leave.

Esaie, though not physically handsome, was as charming as only he could be. He always had the right word to steal a smile from someone no matter how angry he was. Always neat, well-groomed, and well-mannered, he seemed so sure of himself. With a low tone of voice and a contagious smile on his lips, he would look people straight in their eyes and talk to them. Always carrying himself like a perfect gentleman, he exuded confidence.

He was the one handling the outside family affairs. Whether there was a paint job needed or their mother wanted to contact someone, he was the one who did the talking and made the negotiations. Everyone in the neighborhood appreciated him.

No wonder Méralie never stopped complaining about Esaie's popularity. People, mostly women, continuously rang the doorbell or called the housephone asking for him. But the family realized that it was not completely Esaie's fault. Nowadays, if it were not for backup use, the housephones would be obsolete because even the old folks keep their cell phones close wherever they went.

-3-

Around the City

It was 7:00 a.m., and it was cold. According to the forecast, the weather would not go above twenty degrees today. The snow from last night had accumulated to ten feet high. The streets were practically deserted. Even those addicted to their *Jersey Journal* newspaper and coffee did not dare venture out too early.

Anne Marie came out of her room with her hair twisted with large multicolor rollers under a net. She made herself a large cup of tea and sat with her legs tucked under her. All wrapped in a blanket, she was wondering anxiously when the plows would go by although schools would probably be closed. By the window, she watched the timid sun coming out, projecting its first rays shinier than ever over the snow. But it was only to flirt around with that big white blanket because it did not warm up, not even a bit.

Méralie woke up earlier than usual. Not completely recovered from the tiring welcome party, she turned side to side on the bed, rubbing her eyes and trying to take a peek outside through her bedroom window covered with snow.

I haven't seen so much snow in my whole life, she thought. *Definitely* cet hivers est terrible.

With a long robe covering her slippers, she stretched her arms up toward the ceiling and walked out of the door, limping and complaining of her aches and pains. In the kitchen, she made coffee, but the joy and emotion of having her son at home still agitated her.

17

As she sat near the table, looking at the vapors mounted from the cup, thousands of questions assailed her thought, *Where are my nephews? What happened to cousin Laurette? Is Jacqueline alive? How did Hyppolite escape from this disaster?*

In her rush to continue whatever pending conversation from the night before, she went in the boys' room and called Hyppolite, who suddenly jumped out of bed trembling like something terrible was going on.

"What has happened!" he yelled, grabbing his mother's hand. "Not again! Come on! *An allé.*"

"Calm down!" said Méralie, who herself got scared. "Nothing happened. It's about eight o'clock. The coffee is ready."

"I will be out in a moment," said Hyppolite, breathing heavily. "Give me five minutes."

Worried about her son's reaction, Méralie approached Tertulien, who was already sitting in the kitchen.

"I do not understand Popo anymore. He has changed so much. He is not the same pleasant and relaxed man, ready to chat and make jokes like before. He has become a nervous wreck. He is jumpy and always ready to run. I was so surprised to see him sleeping with his clothes on. The pajamas Anne Marie bought him are sitting on the side of the bed, untouched."

"I have a strange feeling something is not right," replied Tertulien. "Hyppolite does not sit down to have a relaxed conversation. Instead, he stands by the door, and while talking, his eyes are staring at the hallway like he fears something. Last night, I gave him the pajamas. He did not want to wear them. I do not know how long I insisted to finally get him to take his shoes off. According to him, we need to be ready at any time in case of an emergency."

"Popo had never been happy due to the fact he was separated from us when he was a kid," replied Méralie with sadness. "But now he is overwhelmed. He is not well. Imagine you are home or in the streets taking care of business, and suddenly, without any warning, the ground starts shaking under your feet. You are losing balance. Houses are collapsing on one side, and people are being crushed to death at the other side. In a matter of seconds, everything is in shambles right before your eyes. Imagine the pain, the suffering of not being able to give a hand to a loved one who is crying desperately for help. Imagine you are running without knowing where you are going."

"Just to hear these words make me shiver. That is worse than a nightmare. It will take him time," said Tertulien, shaking his head, "but I trust in the Lord he will find peace and serenity."

Tertulien and Méralie were still in the kitchen, having their conversation, when Anne Marie came running to them, hands over her head.

"Oh my God!" she yelled, holding a long sheet of paper. "What is this?"

"What is the matter?" asked Tertulien. "What's going on?"

"Take a good look at this bill and tell me if it is possible. It seems that somebody is sitting in the house, making daily phone calls all over the world. Where did all these numbers come from?" said Anne Marie.

"Last month, we made a lot of calls to Haiti, trying to locate our relatives. But all these numbers, I do not know who made these calls."

"I also warned everybody about accepting collect calls. I cannot pay for this gigantic bill!" exclaimed Anne Marie.

"We need to get to a new agreement," said Méralie. "When it comes to bills, life in Jersey City is the same as everywhere in America. Nothing is free. In this house, everyone has a responsibility. I pay the rent. Esaie takes care of any appliance that needs to be fixed or replaced. Anne Marie is responsible for the cable and phone bills, and Tertulien pays the utility bills. But if for any reason, any of the bills goes over the limit, we need to figure out how and get together to solve the problem. As a family, we need to stick to each other and respect the agreement made."

Hyppolite finally came out of his room, and everybody sat around the kitchen table for breakfast. From all the questions he was bombarded with, he spoke about the survivors, people he met after the earthquake; but he was still very reserved about the tragedy itself.

"I do not exactly know how long I will be staying here," he said. "I know everything is in shambles back home. Things will not be okay soon, but I have roots there."

"Tell me about the business. How bad is the situation?"

"It is a total loss. Practically everything is closed. The roof caved in. It is prohibited to get in there. Gertrude and her sister, who used to live next door, are keeping an eye on it. Gertrude was buried for three days under her house. The whole neighborhood got together, and we finally got her out. Thank God she is okay.

"That earthquake taught me things I never knew before. I now understand that fear and desperation can bring people together. Even those who were enemies forgot their differences during that time. More united than ever, the survivors came up as one in a spirit of solidarity, braving more danger to help each other."

"In that moment, it seemed the whole world banded together to help the people in Haiti," said Anne Marie. "The desperation and enormity of the situation has pushed Americans to respond quickly and generously. From what I got from the news, people from all walks of life are helping any way they can. Lots of professionals, including doctors and nurses, made a trip there. They are in place, right in the middle of the disaster, giving a helping hand."

"In Jersey City, the community leaders are doing their best. In city hall, for instance, they are having meeting after meeting with the Haitian community to better understand the situation and help with more efficacy. To us, this is something unforgettable. We will be eternally grateful."

"I was listening to Mommy's conversation," replied Hyppolite. "This family is struggling to keep up with the bills. It is not fair that I become another load for you guys. I need a job, urgently. I must contribute to the expenses, and I also need to help the ones left back home."

"Relax," intervened Méralie. "You got here just last night. Take at least this week to rest and become acquainted with your new life here."

"Mommy is right," said Esaie. "By next week, I will start going around exploring Jersey City, Bayonne, and Secaucus with you in search of employment. The economy is not at its best, but I am confident you will find something. Meanwhile, watch the news. See what's going on, and try improving your English."

The following Tuesday, Anne Marie did not have class. She took advantage to go out with Hyppolite, who was not yet familiarized with the city. Méralie, still enjoying the safe return of her son, went along for a tour in the neighborhood. They drove down to Jewett Avenue and turned to West Side and all the way to Newark Avenue.

"Jersey City has its good side," said Anne Marie. "Life is not bad. These comfortable and gorgeous building were built not long ago. But what you see, it is just the beginning. Lots of changes are going on. For a long time, Jersey City had gone through a tough urban decline that had pushed many of its residents away to the suburbs. But like the sun after a long night of darkness, its bright rays of light come back over the horizon, bouncing back stronger than ever to a new beginning of renaissance. The city is now in full development. It has become a progressive area of commerce, business, new constructions, and style. Modern high-rise buildings are popping up, multiplying all over like mushroom. Nowadays it is a powerful attraction for people looking for modernization and living comfort. Without any doubt, we can proudly say Jersey City is booming.

"Next time, we will visit the Indian store, the Hispanic restaurants, and the Philippine and Italian bakeries."

"It seems that you have people from different backgrounds in the city," said Hyppolite.

"Beside the infrastructure, the architectural marvel of schools and churches, the buildings and offices, the real beauty of the city lies in the diversity of its residents. Boasting one of the most diverse populations in the United States, it is host to an array of ethnicities and cultures. Living up to its legacy as Tapestry of Nations, it counts with people from all over the world. Most of the Latinos established themselves in the Heights. The Indians have their businesses around Journal Square. Lots of Haitians and African Americans occupy the Greenville areas, and the Italians are settled downtown. I am telling you, on late spring and summer days, the streets of Jersey City are like a moving mosaic of beauty, a mobile rainbow of races and ethnicities."

"I do not know about other ethnic groups," intervened Méralie, "but it only takes one Haitian family to settle in a building, then little by little, relatives and friends start grouping around them, and before you know it, the whole neighborhood is filled with people speaking Creole and French."

"That's very interesting," replied Hyppolite, gazing around at the streets.

"With different backgrounds," continued Anne Marie, "people come with their habits and customs, bringing their precious contribution to the great cultural wealth of Jersey City. We greatly appreciate the different tastes and flavors of the ethnic dishes. We'll have time to visit the stores and explore their specialties."

At the light, the car stopped; and from the passenger side, Hyppolite was looking at a display on the side of the street: lots of candles, fresh flowers, balloons, and T-shirts pinned to an electric pole.

"Somebody recently died at this corner," said Anne Marie in response to the inquisitive gaze of her brother.

"This is weird," said Hyppolite, perplexed. "Back home, when car accidents happen, they usually have these kinds of memorials at the place where the departed soul used to live. People would gather for special prayers. What I don't really understand is the T-shirts pinned on the electric poles."

"The T-shirts has the portrait of the person who died, but these deaths are usually gang related. The victims are young people who took the wrong path in life."

From the back seat where she was listening, Méralie felt cold and hot at the same time. Anguish started to build up in the pit of her stomach, crawling up to her throat.

God help us! she thought.

She never expected the conversation to turn that way. So many times, she had walked down the streets, rushing by these kinds of display, with her mind focused only on her church meetings. She knew things happened, but she never asked information or made any connection that some of our youngsters were involved in activities that would push them to go that far. Without saying a word, she went back home with her head pounding.

-4-

Work Gives Independence and Freedom

"Life continues, but it is not always easy," mumbled Meralie with her hands supporting her chin. It is often full of heartache, and things do not always work the way we planned. We need to have a bit of patience and remember that the present situation is not the destination. But when under pressure, the mind is dominated by a fixed idea. We become so stubborn that good advice cannot help much.

Hyppolite was living with a family that was doing everything possible to help him feel better. But attending church, going to the movies, eating out, and visiting Journal Square and the mall were to no avail. In his mind, the only thing necessary was a job. Esaie had tried his best asking him to be patient and relax before thinking about employment, but his convincing power did not work: Hyppolite did not want to hear any reasoning. Facing this situation, the family came under pressure, and Esaie did not have any option but to accede to his brother's petition: they would go job hunting as soon as possible.

As usual, Esaie spent Friday evening ironing and fixing his clothes, getting ready for the whole week.

"Remember to always dress clean and neat," he advised Hyppolite. "In the streets, even in simple clothes, you need to look like a million bucks. We are living in a world so materialistic some people become superficial. When you meet them, before they ask who you are, they focus more on what you look like. So no matter how harsh the situation is, nobody must know your business. 'The dress does not make the monk, but we recognize the monk by his dress.'"

"To be always well-dressed requires a lot of clothes. For that, you need money. Without work, it is quite difficult."

"Let me tell you a secret," said Esaie, lowering his voice as if someone else was listening. "Tertulien and I, before we started working, we used to shop in Newark, Irvington, East Orange, places far away from Jersey City. Those stores sell secondhand clothing in particularly good quality and condition. Without any rush, we would take our time to get what we needed in the right size for a fraction of the money. The rest is a matter of maintenance, keeping your clothes in good shape. You must remember one thing. No matter where you shop or how much you pay, you need to care for your appearance. Decently dressed, a smiling face, and a good posture can take you a long way. It is true some Haitians have a heavy accent, but it is necessary to make yourself understood. There is nothing more important than expressing the right way, finding the right words to address people. Communication is the key to success. Lots of immigrants do have an accent, but they are working. You need to care for your appearance."

Hyppolite, looking at his brother, shook his head. "Can I ask you an indiscreet question?"

"What is it?"

"On three different occasions, I opened the door to some women asking for you. What is going on?"

"I don't have anything to do with those women. Some are confused. You meet them up front. You hold the door and greet them nicely in the hallway. They think about something else. Otherwise, you have to act like a bum all the time."

"What about Yanique?"

"I knew Yanique years ago. Our father was a friend of hers. At that time, we were just kids. Last summer, I met her at a graduation party. Something I do not really understand happened. I was sitting at the bar, drinking a beer and listening to the music, when I started feeling weird. Something I cannot describe was kind of pulling me. When I turned around, she was looking at me with a mysterious gaze that shivered my heart. Dressed in a long white sleeve shirt with a pair of jeans that rested so perfectly on her curved hips, she looked beautiful. I did not recognize her right away. Every time I cast a glance at her, she avoided me, but I know she was looking at me. Finally I went and asked her for a dance. As she did not refuse my invitation, we spent the whole night dancing. She did not want me to take her home, but since then, we kept in touch. I do not know when and how I confessed my love to her. At the beginning, I thought it was a futile relationship, but as time went by, it become more serious. Now, when I meditate about my past, I feel ashamed and do not want to speak about it. I realize that I love her more than anything on earth."

"Were you that bad? What kind of mess are you hiding in your past?" replied Hyppolite, smiling. "It must be terrifying to take a retrospective look at your life."

"This is serious, man," replied Esaie, surprised to see his brother smiling for the first time since he came to Jersey. "Sometimes the road seems wide open you are running wild without paying attention, not even to the reprimand of your loved ones. You are young. You think you got it all. But you need someone special to touch your heart and make you change direction."

"Don't you think she was interested in you before you even declared your love to her? Otherwise, she lives all the way in Bayonne. How did she know so much about you?"

"I don't know, but I was so much in love that I had to reconsider my life, my way of doing things, before approaching her again. She was still in college when she finally accepted me. It was like a new path. A new door had opened to my life. She has touched my soul in such an unusual way that I will not jeopardize the luck that has brought me close to her."

"Lucky you," said Hyppolite. "Love is so delicate. When you finally find it, you need to hold on to it and take good care of it."

The following Monday, bright and early, Esaie and Hyppolite left the house heading to Bayonne in search of employment. They stopped at the new shopping center on Twentieth Street on Route

440. There, they found a line of people already in place waiting to apply for jobs.

"Why so many people?" asked Hyppolite. "This line reminds me of the Port Authority where people were waiting for the bus to New Jersey. Some years ago, when I was here on vacation, it was easier for people to apply for a job."

"The economy is now bad, and a lot of people are out of work. Years ago, life was good. There were plenty of jobs and plenty of everything. America was in great shape. Immigrants were pouring in from all over the world looking for a better life for their children. I remember when the Indians started settling their businesses around Newark Avenue by Journal Square. The good old days! When a lot of Haitians moved into the Greenville area, we were already living at Gifford. But one thing is for sure. The streets were never paved with gold. Lots of people went through awfully hard times before standing on their own feet. And I can tell you nobody had it tougher than the Haitian people."

"What do we do now?"

"We just stand on the line and wait for our turn. Now be positive, relax, and smile. Remember, the first impression stays. The way you present yourself is the way you will be received."

The two men waited a long time, but the line was so long that it did not seem to be moving. It was freezing; Hyppolite was so cold that he could not feel his feet. By noon, they finally grabbed an application and decided to bring it back the next time.

The next day, the two brothers returned to Bayonne and continued their search. The whole week went by; the men cleaned up the Bayonne area—from factory to factory, restaurant to restaurant, and store to store—in search of employment. Many places did not have any opening; instead, they were getting ready to lay people off. Hyppolite had chances to fill out some applications and even had two different interviews. He was told that he would be called when he was needed.

Mohammad, his sister's boyfriend, promised him a job, quick money. But the family had their doubts about that. No one knew what exactly he was doing for a living; he was not trustworthy.

The following week, Tertulien took over. He took Hyppolite to Secaucus and Carlstadt; they went to every possible place where they would find a job. Once more, applications were filled, and promises to be called were made. Hyppolite went home thinking something would come up soon. All he needed was to find whatever job and make some money to deal with the emergency of the moment.

As he sat by the phone impatiently, hoping that a miraculous call would soon bring him the good news, his heart jumped at every ring; but these calls were just women asking for Esaie. As the days passed, Hyppolite became more hermetic and sadder.

"You cannot live like this, my son," said Méralie, approaching him. "You have filled out a lot of applications for employment, and you need to wait until someone calls you. It is only a matter of time. Patience is a virtue, and you need to cultivate the ability to wait without frustration. That will help improve your personality. 'One fire doesn't make dawn.' It is late now. Try to get some sleep. Have good dreams. Relax. Tomorrow will be a better day."

"The reality cannot go away with a dream," replied Hyppolite. "I have already seen the worst. Even in my dreams, I am a frightened man who knows he is about to wake up to a reality worse than a nightmare. At this time, I can only avoid sleeping. I would like to tell myself not to dream at all or, if I do, to dream what is fine, what is beautiful, and okay. But it wouldn't work."

Since the death of Jean Philippe, Tertulien, as the firstborn of the family, felt that he should take more responsibility and care for his mother who was coming up in age. As the company he was working for moved out of the area, he decided to work as a taxi driver. His partner would work during the day, and he would take over in the evening and continue until 2:00 a.m. In the morning, he would be able to keep an eye on his mother while his sister was in school.

He was a cautious man, always trying to plan ahead of time. Since young age, he proved to be disciplined in whatever he accomplished. He had taken his taxi business very seriously—always on time to take over. His was based in Jersey City, but he serviced people all over New Jersey. He had been working as a taxi driver for a long time, and so far, he did not have any accidents or trouble with the police.

One afternoon, he was in the living room talking to Hyppolite, trying to cheer him up; but his brother's mood had become disconcerting. His only subject of conversation was to get a job and take care of business because sitting all day inside the house was stifling. Tertulien was convinced that, if somebody did not do something fast, his brother would lose his sanity. He went to the room to talk to his mother, who was doing her afternoon Bible reading.

"I am concerned about Hyppolite. He does not move away from the phone. He is waiting for calls that may never come. I am observing him. He is getting depressed."

"This is my biggest concern," said Méralie. "I have tried speaking to him, but it is like having a deaf-mute conversation. I don't know what to do."

"I've been thinking," said Tertulien with hesitation. "I would like to take him to work with me this evening, just to distract him for the moment. He will ride around while getting acquainted with his surroundings and breathe some fresh air."

"This is a good idea," replied Méralie. "Instead of sitting here all day, all night, focusing only on problems, the ride will distract his mind. Let us hope he comes back home tired and goes to bed."

It was 5:30 p.m. exactly when Tertulien left the house with Hyppolite. They turned around Journal Square, picked up two passengers, and headed to Irvington. On their way back, they dropped off two other people in Hoboken.

The whole evening, Hyppolite was sitting by his brother, paying attention to his conversation with the clients, checking the name of the streets, watching the traffic, and observing every little detail. He was so focused that one would think he wanted to open his brain and his heart and swallow the whole ritual of the taxi business in one shot. His brother was surprised at his reaction. His expression had changed. The tone of his voice was not the same, and his depressive mood disappeared. He was more into learning than anything else.

Tertulien did not want to disturb him with a long conversation; he limited himself only to answer his questions.

"I have been doing some reading about New Jersey," said Hyppolite. "Do you know why it's also called the Garden State?"

"New Jersey is bathing in the freshness of the Hudson River while offering a breathtaking view of the New York skyline. Between its farms, bearer of the most generous bounties, and its mountains, where giant trees dare to compete with the sky, it is gorgeous. Well-known for its fertile soil and its ability to produce some of the finest fruits and vegetables in the country, this state has a long and distinguished history in which its gardens are a delight for the senses. Wait until spring and summer come. You will appreciate the beauty of its stunning horticultural displays and lush landscapes. Once you pass by the farmers market on Wednesdays, you will discover why it is called the Garden State! Without any exaggeration, it is one of the most beautiful states in the country."

The week went by; Hyppolite looked like a new man. For coming out every evening, he now knew his way around the city and even some parts of the state. Since his clothes were always pressed and in good shape, he did not have any problem following Esaie's advice: simply dressed but look like a million bucks. Soon he became the right hand of his brother, supporting him, watching out for him, and even offering him advice and help.

The whole household also felt the goodness of that change. His continued animation and interest had brought a breath of fresh air to Méralie, who has not stopped lifting her hands, giving thanks to the Lord. She did not understand the change in her son, but it came like a blessing, a divine miracle.

The fact is that inactivity is the worst enemy of Hyppolite. He was only twenty-seven years old, healthy, and full of energy. Raised in Haiti by his grandmother, a highly active businesswoman, he was taught since a young age that manna does not fall from the sky anymore but *work gives independence and freedom*. He was a teenager when he started helping his grandmother with the family business. In fact, he was the only one she trusted.

Right after college, he opened his own warehouse and had people working for him even on Sundays. Untiring, he was always on the go, struggling to make things work. After the earthquake that had left the whole country in chaos, he was forced to join his family in the United States, leaving everything behind. So sitting at his mother's house day after day, looking at the streets through the window, was driving him crazy. Now, going out with his brother—rocking the streets, beating the traffic, avoiding accidents, and being mindful of people getting in and out of the taxi—was the best therapy. That was the button that rang his bell—the wake-up call that pulled him out of his lethargy.

On Sundays, Méralie and Anne Marie usually left for church by 8:30 a.m. Although Hyppolite was not a fervent Christian, he had planned to accompany his mother that weekend; but when he came out of his room, it was already nine o'clock. He was about to join his brothers who were sitting in the kitchen talking to each other. He stopped at the sound of the bell to answer the door. It was Takeema, the lady who lived across the street. Esaie immediately went to his room, pretending that he was not home. Hyppolite followed him to remind him about their last conversation when he said that he was not interested in any woman in the neighborhood. But before he even said anything, Esaie intervened.

"I met this woman six years ago in Newark. We had a relationship for a short period of time. Every single weekend, she wanted to go out for the whole night. She smokes more than a chimney. I could not keep up. Suddenly she took off with another man, and I never saw her again. The other day, I was coming home when I noticed her in front of the building. To my surprise, she told me she just moved across the street. I told her clearly that I have someone in my life, but it seemed that she does not care. Now she knows when I go out and when I am home. She is always in front of the building watching my every move. The worst part of it is that she is living with someone who is suspicious. The man thinks that she has something going on with me."

-5-

A Special Bouquet

"Life is beautiful when you are young and healthy," said Méralie, thinking out loud in front of the calendar attached to the wall. "Surrounded by family and friends, you have no worries. You are happy. While walking, you hit the ground strong. You breathe free and take every step with confidence. You are filled with the joy of living. You can do it all. No mountain is too high nor trouble too difficult to overcome. You become a fountain of energy, feeling like spreading your wings and touching the sky. At least that is the way it should be at this magical stage of life."

Soon a sound of music coming from her daughter's room filled the whole house. It was still early morning; the rest of the family wasn't up yet. Méralie was about to knock at the bedroom's door, demanding to turn down the radio, but instead she turned around and went back to the kitchen, smiling.

That Wednesday morning, Anne Marie was up earlier than usual.

Happier than ever, she was singing and moving along to the beat, "If he like it, then he better put a ring in it!"

Dressed in a pair of boots up to her knees, a red scarf, and a hat covering her forehead and ears, she was ready to confront the windy and cold weather like a valiant soldier. By 8:00 a.m., she was already out, heading to Hudson Community College via Bergen Avenue.

Méralie also woke up early with a well-designed plan for the day. In fact, the whole household got together to make it an incredibly special one. It had been twenty-one years since the birth of the only baby girl of the family, twenty-one years since Anne Marie's arrival had brought immense joy to their home.

When Méralie got married, her greatest desire was to have a girl, a little princess who would complete her happiness. But her first child was a boy. She kept on trying and kept on having boys until eight years later when she finally gave birth to a baby girl. Since then, Anne Marie had been the center of attention. She had robbed the heart and affection of the whole family. And precisely around her birthday was the time when Méralie thought more about her late husband, who had loved their daughter more than himself. She came out of her room fixing her scarf over her head, ready to do everything on her part to make this birthday a happiest one.

Today is the day that God has made. Let's rejoice in it.

At the same time, her multitasking mind was going back and forth to other thoughts. She could not help thinking that some of the kids did not have a happy and quiet birthday or a mother around to celebrate with them—the kids who were living the monotony of life with the same routine of violence, cursing, and running wild day after day. Since she became more aware of the shrines often displayed at the sidewalks, Méralie had been paying more attention while walking down the streets. She even stopped to look at those T-shirts hanging at the outside walls. She felt a kind of bitterness, an unstated pain moving her heart.

"These kids are so young. They've already taken the wrong path. I do not want to criticize them, spew out venom upon them. They have enough problems as it is. They are facing a world that is cold, that is dark. They do not know what to do. They do not know where to turn to. Many of them are tormented, their hearts broken. They are thrown away and cast off. I think the best way to come through without the bondage and the pressure ensnaring them, trying to destroy them, is to turn themselves to God."

As she was moving around, she started humming a song, trying to push away the painful thoughts; for it was not a day to be sad. By 11:30 a.m., she was already in the kitchen preparing a special dinner for the occasion. She had always been a good cook, but when it came to Haitian food, she was a star. The delicious aroma of her macaroni gratiné, *riz aux chevrettes*, was a phenomenon that would pull the neighbors in like a magnet.

At 1:00 p.m., the bell rang, and a huge bouquet was delivered to the house with a note. Since Anne Marie was still in school, Méralie, in her curiosity, grabbed the card and peeked.

Dear Annie,

I would like to strip the Jersey City gardens of their most beautiful roses. I would like to steal the sweetest notes from the most romantic music and collect the brightest stars from the Haitian sky that never knew the winter season to make a special bouquet today, the day of your birth. Since time and distance are failing me, please accept these roses with my heart that is beating only for you.

Benoit

Méralie went back to the kitchen thinking out loud, "This young man is such a nice and handsome human being. No matter how long he had been living or was born in America, he is a native-natal Haitian, a perfect gentleman. He has manners. With pleasure, I would welcome him in my family, but Anne Marie is still in school. It is too early for all of this. Besides, there is Mohammad, who does not let go of her. Wherever she goes, he is right there! He is attached to her like glue! Something tells me that he is not a good man."

Everything was ready for the celebration at dinnertime. The house had flowers in every corner. Everyone looked happy and relaxed. Tertulien and Esaie came back home early; Hyppolite joined them. Joseph made it from Paterson. Edmond, the boy from down the street, also attended. Anne Marie met him randomly three weeks ago. One day, while coming home from the library, she noticed a young boy sitting on her stoop; he was about Joseph's age. He looked like he belonged there. As they kept on speaking, she brought him home for dinner. Since then, Méralie embraced him as another grandson. According to her, Edmond looked exactly like Hyppolite when he was his age.

By 4:00 p.m., Anne Marie came back home with Mohammad, who picked her up at school. Dressed up for the occasion, he had a brand-new pair of jeans and jacket on, the most expensive ones but his own style. While waiting for Anne Marie, who went to the kitchen, he lit a cigarette; and Méralie did not take long to show her disapproval.

"Please, could you remind Mohammad that he has to go outside to smoke? Because we don't use any ashtrays in the house."

To the comment, nobody responded. Anything sounding negative went unnoticed. The last twenty-one years had gone so fast all the focus had to be on the birthday girl. There was motive only for celebration, so everybody needed to cooperate to make it a truly special and fabulous day.

Anne Marie was a young woman with a smile that reminded of the rising sun. She was tall but reasonably proportioned: her long legs and small waistline gave her the Coca-Cola shape so venerated by the Haitian men. Besides, she had that special charm and grace that enhanced her imposing beauty. Gentle and well-mannered, she was a vision of loveliness. Anyone would take her for a fragile and delicate girl, but not at all. She was an athlete. She joined the basketball team during her high school years, and she was particularly good at it. Also, being the only girl growing among her brothers and their neighborhood's friends, she had developed a passion for martial arts, most specifically the judo. That evening, she wore an exotic blue dress that fell just beneath her knees. The laces across the bodice made it fit so perfectly. To that, she added the prettiest silver earrings that seemed to just sparkle from within. She was splendid!

Yanique, Esaie's fiancée, did not want to miss the party. She came straight from work to greet the birthday girl. She brought her a precious gift, a book titled *Crossing Treacherous Path,* a novel that gave a good insight into the country of Haiti.

"Happy birthday," she said, putting the book in Anne Marie's hands. "You were born in the United States of America," she said, "but it's always good to know about your ancestors, your roots."

Hyppolite was going through some personal issues, but he could not stay indifferent to his sister's birthday. He had always been an eloquent man. He had a special thirst for knowledge. Back in high school, he used to pass time in the library, collecting general information on literature and culture. His friends gave him the nickname "the intellect." Through his actual and apparent poise, he did not need time to prepare a speech. He was one of those men who, at any circumstance or time, was not scared to stand in front of a crowd. With assurance, the words would flow out of his lips like a melody to charm his audience. Everybody was in the living room congratulating Anne Marie when he approached his sister and gave her a big hug.

"Twenty-one years ago," he said, "a bright star was born, and my grandmother Emma predicted that it would make the whole family shine. As I am looking at you today, I cannot stop thinking about her. She was a strong, intelligent, and hardworking woman. She was beautiful, flirtatious, proud, *une femme totale,* but transparent and sincere. She was a woman who stood tall with a gaze that reflected the love and compassion she had in her soul. You have her posture. You inherited her energy. And our father would have been so thrilled, so happy, tonight. The baby, the girl of his heart, has turned twenty-one years old. Unfortunately, he has gone too early. God rest his soul.

"Tonight there is joy. There is happiness in the air," continued Hyppolite. "We gather to celebrate our sister's birthday. It seems like yesterday when she came into our lives and captivated us all. Our baby sister is now a woman. That little rose bulb has blossomed to a beautiful flower!

"Little sister, today is your day. Dance like no one's watching. Sing like no one's listening. Love like you will never get hurt, and live like its heaven on earth! I can tell you that twenty-one is the magic number. It is the perfect age. You will see *la vie en rose,* but unfortunately it is not forever. The other day, I was visiting the Newport Mall, and I saw a store with a very peculiar name that made me stop and think for a while, Forever 21.

"My darling sister, you are twenty-one only once and right now. Life is full of promises. It is beautiful. It is in front of you. Go

35

for it without hesitation or pause. As you continue your trajectory, make sure you have more dreams than memories, more opportunities than chances, more hard work than luck, and more friends than acquaintances.

"You are so full of life, fresh like morning dew. You are more beautiful than all the roses decorating this apartment. Enjoy your day to the max and be happy. May you have the absolute best. I speak for the whole family as I wish you a happy birthday."

In a round of applause, kissing, and hugging, everybody held hands; and in a perfect harmony, they lifted their voices to a melodious birthday tune:

> Bon anniversaire
> Nos vœux les plus sincères
> Que ces quelques fleurs
> Vous apportent le bonheur
> Que l'année entière
> Vous soit douce et légère
> Et que l'an fini
> Nous soyons tous réunis
> Pour chanter en chœur
> Bon anniversaire

*****

> Happy birthday
> Our most sincere wishes
> May these flowers
> Bring you happiness
> May the whole year
> Be sweet and light
> And may at the end of it
> We all get together again
> So let sing in concert
> Happy birthday

Anne Marie was so happy; she was moved to tears. Unfortunately, she could not enjoy the rest of the evening with the family. By six thirty, she left with Mohammad because they had planned to go out.

"She should have stayed here with us," said Esaie. "That man is a pain. He doesn't convince me. If he had more understanding, he would encourage her to stay with the family. They would go out on Sunday."

"I don't understand Anne Marie and this man," said Méralie. "Since the day they laid eyes on each other, it is like their fate was sealed. They are inseparable. Wherever Anne Marie goes, Mohammad follows. Once she is home, the phone is glued to her ears until she falls asleep. It is like the family has passed to the second row"

Listening to his mother, Hyppolite shook his head, smiling, "Please, no reproach today. She is twenty-one. Let's be happy for her."

It seems Méralie did not understand that babies do not stay babies forever. They grow; they open their eyes to life and eventually their hearts to love. And love is so unpredictable and so inexplicable. Sometimes it goes beyond our understanding. Human beings need to love and to be loved. They need to love freely with all their hearts without being scared to be misunderstood. And the reciprocity of love between a man and a woman is one of the principal joys of life.

Everybody was still in the living room with the radio on when the phone rang. It was Marie Louise, Joseph's mother, complaining.

"Joseph is acting out. He got suspended from school for lack of discipline. He does not listen. He does not follow orders. In the house, he considers his stepfather as his enemy. He is talking back to him. Instead of doing his homework, he is sitting outside with friends. He got upset because he did not get the cell phone he had been asking for."

"I do not want to give him any cell phone," replied Tertulien, "at least not now. He would just be talking to his friends all day long instead of studying."

"When we had only housephones, parents were able to have more control over their children," remarked Méralie. "At least they were speaking with their friends inside the home. You had an idea of what they were saying, but not anymore. Nowadays they go out the door with their cell phone to speak, and God knows who they are talking to. After ten o'clock at night, kids were not allowed to pick up the phone. If a friend called late at night, you were able to control that, but not anymore. These days, anybody can wake up your kids at any time. You do not even know it."

"You are being antitech, Mommy," said Hyppolite. "Adaptation is the principle of survival. Times have changed. We are living a new era. Technology is moving in gigantic steps. We need to keep up with it, or we will fall behind."

"Besides," continued Méralie, "who did not pay much attention to her son? It seems that everybody is crazy. They are walking alone in the streets talking nonstop. You would think they are talking to themselves. On top of that, you have the internet, social media, etc. that makes it even more difficult to know what the kids are doing. Technology is incredibly good, but it also has its dark side."

"I do not like this man around my son," said Tertulien, upset. "He drinks. He smokes, and he is not treating him well. He is a bad influence. I would like to have Joseph with me for good, but Marie Louise won't give me custody."

"It would be good if Joseph could stay here with us," said Méralie. "He is an incredibly talented boy. He has such a nice voice. I like when he sings in the choir. If he stays here with us for good, he will find more encouragement from church, and he would be more involved in the meetings and youth rehearsals. I always take a real pleasure watching the church youth choir perform. What a harmony, what strength in their voice! Standing tall, straight, their hair black like raven wings, the spring of youth still on their cheek but praising the Lord with such fervor, they fire up the whole congregation."

The next day, Anne Marie went back to class with a radiant smile. But as she was showing her friend Raquel the pictures taken on her birthday, she expressed a bit of concern.

"I went out with Mohammad and came back by eleven only to be assaulted with questions. The whole family was sitting in the living room waiting for me. They want to know who his parents are, if he is still in school, the kind of studies he has done, what he does for a living, etc. It really hurts to know they do not like him at all. I feel like my mother would prefer that I love someone else."

"If you want my advice," continued Raquel, "it's better you don't tell Mohammad all of this. You do not want to create any animosity among the people you love."

"I spoke to him on the phone this morning. He already knew everything."

"When people are young and in love," said Raquel, "they often pass out a lot of little details to focus more on the relationship itself. You need loved ones who care to watch out for you and make sure you are not mistaken. Now did you answer these questions? How well do you know this man?"

"I cannot believe what I am hearing!" said Anne Marie. "Are you trying to tell me my family should choose a man for me? Do you believe in arranged marriages? As a young woman, you sound worse than my mother. Let me tell you. We are not in seventeenth century anymore. I am a twenty-first-century woman. I have freedom. I can work, make my own money, and choose my own man. I know what is most important about Mohammad. He is a hardworking man, a good man. He loves me, and I trust him."

Anne Marie was not too happy with the conversation, but Raquel piqued her curiosity and got her thinking. Mohammad always spoke about his big connections, like friends and business partners that she never met. He was making money, but she did not know exactly where he was working. He had been nice to her, but she could not ignore that he had a temper. She recalled the first time he picked her up at lunch break. They walked from her school over to the White Castle. Right when they were about to enter the restaurant, a homeless man approached them and asked for some change. She got chills every time she thought about how Mohammad chased him away, cursing and screaming threats. Now she wondered how he would react if he felt that the relationship was being threatened by the disapproval of the family.

That afternoon, he picked Anne Marie up as usual and took her home. They stood on the front porch; he did not want to go inside.

"Your family does not like me. I feel their rejection. Your brothers are doing all this because they think they are geniuses, that they are above it all. Maybe they want a rich man or a genius like Hyppolite. They think that I am not good enough for you."

"Hyppolite is not a genius, and my family cannot make any choices for me. They will accept you. They do not have any choice. You are working, and you are studying. I must speak to them."

"I think no matter the studies I would have done, the amount of money I would be making, or whatever family I would have come from would make your family like me or accept me as your fiancé. Their opinion about me was formed since the first day they saw me, and that really hurts. I would not care if I did not really love you, but I do."

"I was talking to my friend Raquel in school today. She advised me to do things right. You have been visiting me for a while now. My family knows that you and I love each other, but they have been asking a lot of questions because they do not know anything about you. I think you should at least speak to my mother. We need to do things the proper way. My brothers are putting pressure on me."

"I don't know exactly what they want to know about me, but no matter what happens, I want you to understand I love you. You are wrapped tightly around my heart. You take my breath away. You are the most beautiful thing that has ever happened to my life. I feel I cannot live without you. I will love you forever."

"Listen," said Anne Marie, holding his face with her hands. "Look at me. No one will separate us. Our love will conquer it all. I love my family very much, but I love you too. They will have to understand that."

Between promises, confessions, and the attraction they had for each other, they joined their lips in a kiss that seemed never ending. And precisely at the exact moment, Tertulien, coming from work, walked up the front steps and surprised them.

"What is going on here? I want to have a talk with Mohammad. Anne Marie, please go inside."

"But we were not doing anything wrong," said Anne Marie, who ran upstairs, upset.

"Mohammad," said Tertulien, "what exactly do you think you are doing out here with my sister? You have been coming over, visiting Anne Marie as a friend, and no one has a problem with that. She is not a prisoner. But there is not a single person in this family that would accept a spectacle like this. You have never spoken to anyone—not my brothers, my mother, or me—about having an interest in her. This family doesn't know you."

"I love Anne Marie with all my heart. I will do whatever it takes to make her happy. We were speaking about going to Mrs. Méralie just before you came in."

"Anne Marie just turned twenty-one. She is still in school. She needs to study and have a career before thinking about any relationship. It is too early for that."

"I am not disturbing her in any way. I always encouraged her to study and pursue her career."

"If you really love her, please leave her alone. Let her breathe. It is true Anne Marie is not a baby anymore, but she is not matured yet to sustain a serious relationship. You are both young, impulsive. You are acting without thinking, and this is a good recipe for disaster. Lord knows who else you have out there."

"I would never do anything to hurt Anne Marie."

"Please! What I just saw, what is it? Kissing in the front porch where everybody is coming in and out is not enough. We don't even know much about you."

Tertulien did not want to hear any more explanation; he ended the conversation and went back upstairs.

Upset and frustrated, Mohammad did not know what to do. He came out of the building and stood on the sidewalk, thinking. Some friends passed by and waved at him; he did not pay attention. He was looking at them but did not even see anyone; his mind was elsewhere. As he was convinced that they would never accept him in the family, he became worried.

The way this is going, I will have to rob her and disappear from Jersey City. After all, my relationship is not with them.

While standing out there lost in his thoughts, he noticed Esaie walking quickly from the corner of Martin Luther King Drive. toward him; he looked angry. Next to him walking just as fast but smiling and talking was Takeema, the woman who lived across the street. Esaie stopped abruptly under a tree about five feet away.

Mohammad just listened and watched as Esaie, through clenched teeth, told the woman, "Stop speaking to me! I am sorry. If you cannot understand that, then…I don't know!"

He abruptly turned around and proceeded over to the building. As he came face-to-face with Mohammad, he paused as a sign of embarrassment, choked a bit, and continued silently up the stairs.

Perplexed and a bit confused, Mohammad was looking at him walking away.

What is Esaie doing in the streets, arguing with that woman? he thought. *Not even fifteen minutes ago, Tertulien was making a speech of perfect gentlemen, showing the members of his family as the most honest and impeccable, a family for which kissing on the front porch is considered as a terrible sin. Humph! But the facts are saying the opposite. Who is the bad guy?*

Mohammad went across the street in search of information. The only thing he wanted was to discover a mistake, something he could use to slow down these men who thought he was not good enough for Anne Marie. He decided not to let it go, and it seemed he would have an alliance with Takeema.

-6-

A Glimpse of Hope

Hyppolite, for being raised away from the family, did not have enough faith to be a fervent Christian. According to him, life is simple: we are born, we grow, and we die. There is no such thing as destiny or luck. Whatever happens is just mere coincidence, nothing more. That is all anything ever is. A faithful, religious woman as Méralie would claim a divine miracle for any good thing that happened: God is directing our steps, and everything has a purpose in life. We may not understand it, but nothing happened without the permission of God.

But there are situations or circumstances that coincide so perfectly, if they were not miracles, no one would know what they are.

Esaie was working as a bank teller in South Jersey. The week following the family meeting, he was sitting at his desk when the assistant manager came in with a flyer announcing a van for sale. The van belonged to his brother, who did not have use for it. Since Esaie was the only one in the office that showed interest in the van, they decided to sell it to him. He thought it was a perfect idea; the van would come in handy. Hyppolite was an intelligent and responsible man; he would occupy himself with something. To him, a phone call was not good enough to break the news. All optimistic, he took half a day off, went back home, and got the family together.

"What I have to say is important. Your opinion is crucial in this matter because it is up to you to make it a reality. The manager of my job is selling a van in good condition. I made a deal with him

43

thinking about Hyppolite. I would like to have your opinion about him working as a self-employed driver."

"That would be a blessing if Popo could occupy himself in something profitable," intervened Anne Marie, "but I am worried, though, about this job."

"Hyppolite came here devastated," said Esaie. "We all understand why. Then sitting in the house all day long thinking about what happened was not helping. Since the first day he went on the road with Tertulien, a sudden change happened. In the beginning, I thought it was a mood swing, the excitement of the moment. But as the time is passing by, he stood by my brother going out every day, learning, helping. With his ideas, Tertulien improved his business procedures. I think this is a good sign. He has a lot of potential to work a steady job and even to work as a taxi driver."

"Do you really think so?" said Méralie, relieved. "Does he know the streets enough? Does he have the mind for a job like that?"

"Yes," intervened Tertulien, "he knows the streets. He is a highly active man. He is going through some difficulties, but he has discipline. In the beginning, I was surprised and a bit hesitant to see how well he handled some situations. But so far, he has demonstrated that he was not acting under stress or emotion, but he really has talent and intelligence for the business."

"We know that driving a taxi is not as easy as everyone thinks. There are some steps to take to be in conformity with the law. Besides, the competition with other cabdrivers is high. It is a jungle out there!"

"All of this is because of the job situation out there," said Anne Marie, scared by the idea of her brother driving alone all day long. "He could have gotten a regular job, but instead of hiring, companies upon companies are letting people go, or worse, they are declaring bankruptcy. Unemployment is soaring. Politicians promise you a heaven with God when they need your vote. Now they are nowhere to be found. People are suffering. They cannot pay their bills. Their assets are going down the drain. The unemployment, welfare, and Social Security offices are overwhelmed. The claimants' lines are growing like grass in water. The temp agencies cannot handle their caseload."

"Hold it right here, young lady!" yelled Méralie, upset. "How many times have I said that I do not want any conversation about politics in my house?"

"I am surprised that you have that position about politics," replied Anne Marie. "You have been in America for so long working at the courthouse, rubbing shoulders with politicians daily."

"Politics are too dangerous. I know what I am talking about."

"This is typical of the Haitian people. They hear the word *politics*, and they panic. For this reason, they fear the polls. They do not vote. Even for the census, they hide themselves. I think that is a shame. The Haitian people are hard workers. They are taxpayers. Someone needs to do something to get them informed. They must know it is not a sin or a crime to speak out. They need to get themselves involved. They need to know that, if they do not participate in the community's social and political events, their voice will not be heard. No vote, no voice!"

"Yes, indeed!" approved Esaie.

"We were talking about Hyppolite, weren't we?" observed Tertulien, who seemed to agree with his mother's ideas.

"Okay, okay," said Anne Marie, "we cannot dwell forever on this situation. Due to his nervous condition, I would rather see my brother occupy himself with something else instead of being a cabdriver. But since there are not any other options, let us be objective. He is an American citizen. He already has a license, and he is taking a CDL class. So far, it is a good beginning. Now tell us what else he needs. What is the next step?"

"Hyppolite is not crazy, if that is what you are trying to say," intervened Tertulien. "He is just frustrated because he cannot find a job. We need to get the van before they sell it to someone else. I have some savings, but it will not be enough."

Everybody was scratching their head, thinking they would have to contribute to the extent of their capability. Armed with pen and paper, Esaie was monitoring the situation, calculating how much a down payment would be needed for a decent loan.

At that point, Hyppolite opened the door and found everyone gathered around the kitchen table.

"What is going on? Another meeting?"

"We are talking about your CDL classes."

"I thank you all for everything you are doing for me," said Hyppolite, annoyed. "I know every one of you care very much. But I do not appreciate that you are having meeting after meeting about me without even telling *me* anything. I am a grown man. You cannot decide my life for me. I know, for the moment, I depend on you for a lot of things, but I am not incapacitated."

"I am sorry you think like this. We all know that you are not a child, far from it."

"Sometimes we depend on people, like a mirror, to define us, to tell us who we are," said Hyppolite. "But whether the reflection is encouraging or not, if it is about me, I would like to know it. If you have an opinion or something to say, please let me know it. Do not hesitate to talk to me."

"Okay. We are about to make a good deal. We just want to make sure we have something concrete before we put any idea in your mind. We do not want you to be disappointed in case it does not work."

"Be more specific. What kind of deal are you talking about?"

"My assistant manager offered me a van in good condition. His father purchased it new. One year later, he became sick and could not use it. When he passed away, he left it to his other son who is selling it. Imagine, this van has been sitting in their garage for at least two years, and precisely at this moment, when you are looking for something, they put it up for sale. Today they brought the flyers in. Half of the office is out because of the snowstorm. Since I am the only one interested, they are trying to facilitate me the deal. If we got this van, it would be perfect for business. What a happy coincidence! I think this deal is a godsend."

"Slow down," said Hyppolite. "It is all right to be enthusiastic, but before you get too excited, you need to study the facts. This is an investment. You cannot act under pressure or with emotion. You must calculate and balance the pros and cons. Even though you saw the van and it looks new, that does not mean it is in good condition.

"First what year is the van? Did it ever have any accidents? Before we talk about tune-up and an oil change, it is important that a mechanic check it out. Secondly, if you are going to get a loan, how much will the monthly payments be? Can we afford it? What kind of business do you have in mind? What is your jurisdiction? Did you target your clientele?"

While Hyppolite was completing the CDL class, he guided his brother step-by-step through the whole process of negotiation. Thanks to his support, the deal was a success.

The acquisition of the van was not only an investment for business but the miracle breakthrough the family was begging for. Hyppolite might have been a sensitive and even an emotional man, but he was a fighter. He was raised by his grandmother in a place where honey and milk were not abundant. The catastrophic event from January had taken a big toll on him. In a matter of minutes, he had lost friends and family; his life savings and investments were gone. It is understood he could be down for a time. But like a plant wilted by dryness regaining vitality on contact with water, he had that gracious faculty to bounce back from any situation as soon as a glimpse of hope showed up on the horizon.

He started to drive the van. His brother accompanied him for two days, observing and guiding him. The first day while riding around, they ended up in downtown Jersey City by the waterfront. They had been downtown before but not all the way there. Hyppolite was observing the area. He could not put his head down, looking at the high-rise buildings erected straight up like they were confronting the sky. The tremendous movement of the people rushing in and out of the buildings and the ups and downs of the bus riders warmed the air with activity and vitality. In front of one building, he got out of the van to observe better. To satisfy his brother's curiosity, Tertulien told him about the whole history at once.

"This area," he said, "was previously occupied by rail yards and factories. In the 1980s, they began the development of this water-front, then the rapid construction of these high-rise buildings led to the development of the Exchange Place financial district, also known as Wall Street West, one of the largest banking centers in the United States. Presently a lot of large financial institutions occupy these mar-velous edifices that are among the tallest building in New Jersey."

Hyppolite was listening to his brother, but his eyes were going around observing his surroundings. He marveled at the sight.

"The inbound and outbound buses remind me of the Port Authority. This place is incredible. These buildings rival the sky-scrapers in Manhattan. People living in Jersey City should be proud."

The third day, Hyppolite did not go out. As a man who had been dealing with all kinds of business since young age, he spent most of the day thinking, preparing his strategy to launch his activity.

Looking at him writing, drawing lines, and making diagrams, Esaie said, laughing, "My God! This is not a simple delivery-service business. You are making plan for an enterprise."

"The idea," he said, "is not running around, burning fuel without knowing where you are going. Some contacts need to be made. There are some strategic points at certain times of the day that need to be known before you hit the streets."

The family, including the brothers, trusted his good judgment and hoped for the best.

All optimistic and enthusiastic, Hyppolite started on the right foot. Intoxicated by the promises of the business, he embraced the job with all his heart and strength, hoping that his expectation would align with reality. At first, he limited his working area to Jersey City. Little by little, he started to gain experience with the streets and get used to some customers, and he enlarged his jurisdiction to more of Hudson County.

By the first week, the monthly payment of the van was ready. He usually started at six o'clock in the morning, came back home at noon, and went back out at 2:00 p.m. until the evening. Early in the morning, he took some factory workers to Secaucus and Carlstadt and picked them up in the evening. Some kids in the neighborhood were attending St. Patrick's, Sacred Heart, and St. Mary's school. He planned with parents for their transportation.

Through one of his customers, he met Hellen, a woman who was working in a law firm downtown. She was on the phone with her aunt, who was riding in the van coming from work, when her car broke down. Hyppolite nicely agreed to help until she fixed the car. He just had to pick her up in Secaucus in the morning and take her back in the evening.

Hellen and Hyppolite's first meeting was very impressive. Neat and clean as usual, he was waiting for her at the exact time in front of her office. As she came out, he introduced himself and offered his hand to help her into the van. The simple contact of their hands produced a kind of mysterious and silent reaction that surprised both; electricity seemed to pulsate through their bodies. The week went by; Hellen was fascinated by the way Hyppolite carried himself and interacted with people. On two different occasions he went to drop her home in the afternoon, she invited him in for coffee. They got to know each other better, and from these casual meetings was born a kind of relationship that seemed to be going beyond friendship.

Hellen was around thirty years old. She was married at twenty-two to a lawyer and lived in Florida. After her divorce, she moved to Secaucus and had been living alone for five years. When she met Hyppolite, his well-mannered ways, his gentlemanly kindness, and even his heavy French accent got her attention. She felt there was something mysterious about him, something more than she could see. And that so-called mystery led her to the strong attraction she felt for him.

Hyppolite was not indifferent at all to the affection she was cultivating. He had accompanied her sometimes to the movies but was hesitant. When he remembered the ordeal he went through and the people he left behind, he felt guilty for having any good and peaceful times when others were still suffering bitterly. More discreet, he kept quiet and did his best to cover up; but deep inside, he was at war against his own feelings.

Hellen was an attractive woman. The immaculate skin of her beautiful face and a smile bigger than the morning sun were an obsession. Her luscious red lips opening on a set of white and shiny teeth reminded you of red and juicy apples that you would only find at the farmers market. To Hyppolite, she was the most beautiful woman in all of creation; she was an angel fallen from the sky. Every time he cast a nervous glance at her, he caught her looking at him. And when she glanced away, she was like a statue posing for appreciation. In his mind, only one question kept coming to torment him, How would a kiss from this woman be?

When dropping her home in the evening, he had the habit of stopping the van completely and watching her walk until she entered the house and closed the door behind her. All these cautionary measures were not for any security reason as he was claiming. He was simply fascinated with Hellen and would rather take advantage that she turned her back to see her walking and admire her at a certain distance. In fact, her only presence was a reason of tension; whether it was close or at a distance, any encounter with her made him sweat. But shyness and the memory of his recent tragedy stopped him from expressing himself.

Always smiling with his gentlemanly manners, he had succeeded in covering up his feelings quite well. But the truth was Hyppolite was like a twelve-ounce foam cup: quiet and cold from the outside, but the inside was like a coffee in ebullition that couldn't stand its own heat.

One afternoon while driving her home, Hellen was looking at him and was thinking, *Since I have been living in this area, this man is the only one for whom I feel such an absorbing passion. I know he is not indifferent to me. I see it in his eyes. When he is smiling at me, they are smiling along. But what stops him to make the first step? Does he have a family? Why is he so mysterious? What is possibly going on?*

As they got to Secaucus, Hellen tried to speak to him.

"Since we have met, I have been talking about my life and everything else. But I do not know much about you. It is true some men do not like to speak about their lives, but you, you are so tightly closed you are a mystery. Tell me about you. Do you have any kids?"

"No, I do not have any. I am not married," said Hyppolite.

"Since I left Florida," continued Hellen, "I have been living in this area. With my kind of job, I meet people every day, but you are so different. You never talk about any women. It seems something powerful is restraining you from love. What is it?"

"You will never know how difficult it is for me to express my feelings. I must confess that I feel good and at peace when I am at your side. Your goodness has brought me calmness, has revived something I thought I would never feel again. I don't know what to say. Yes, I do love you, but because of that, I feel that I am a poor, selfish, miserable creature."

"Did it ever come to your mind that things could be worse? You could also have died in that tragedy. I know you do not believe in fate, but if you went through so much and you are still alive without any injury, don't you think it is for some reason? Maybe you do not know yet what your mission in life is. You will never forget the friends and family you lost in that earthquake. Their memory will stay in your heart, but you need to learn to let go. Do not let the remembrance of the past or the anxiety of the future cripple today's opportunity. You have potential. You are an intelligent man. Life goes on."

"They say, when a loved one dies, a part of you dies with him," replied Hyppolite. "After the tragedy that had killed so many of my loved ones, I don't know how much is left of me."

Part 2
The Package

———————————————

———————————

Life is not always as easy as it sounds
But it is what it is
The world sometimes bears down awfully hard
Pick up your strength from wherever
Don't you dare give up

We all make mistakes and regret afterward.
We need to acknowledge the suffering, push forward
while aiming and striving for a better situation.
No matter how clear seems to be the horizon,
obstacle often comes from opposite direction,
bringing days that are filled with frustration.
But whatever the challenge you must face,
do not let anxiety and fear trouble your peace.
Sometimes it takes a storm to find a secure place.
If the road is bumpy and muddy, do not race.
To get to the right exit, you need to stay the pace.
Hold your head high and keep on smiling.
Do not aim to lose; keep on hoping.
The struggle you are in today is an adventure
to the path for a better future.

-7-

The Discovery

In the family, things started to look up. Since Hyppolite started to work, somehow the pressure was off, and Méralie seemed to recover the peace of mind so anticipated. Hyppolite himself was surprised by the impulses of his heart. He did not know when exactly he had quit his bitterness and opened to a feeling more pleasant but not less tormented. He could not stop thinking about Hellen's gaze, the way she looked straight at him. Her clear and bright eyes made him feel that he was being scrutinized under an x-ray machine.

Damn! he thought. *Would she pick up my senses? Would she know the daily fight I am having with my own heart? Can she read my mind? I wish I met her in a different time, a different occasion. I wish the circumstances were different. All would be so perfect.*

Indeed, all seemed to be perfect. The family was happy; Hyppolite became more jovial and more pleasant. The relief was almost complete. This was a dream come true. The only cloud on the horizon was that he was not yet over with sleeping with his clothes on. He would come home in the evening and take his shower but get dressed again before going to bed.

Anne Marie came home from school as usual with her inseparable Mohammad. He did not want to go inside because Esaie was already home, and they did not get along too well. Nevertheless, Mohammad was like a shadow that never quit. Very often, when bringing her home in the evening, long after Anne Marie went inside, he would stay in front of the building or in the vestibule, like he was watching her sleep. Sitting on the steps playing a harmonica, he would stay there for hours before going back to his own place. In the beginning, the residents of the building were nervous to see him there all the time. But since he never caused any disturbance, they got used to him. Some ladies even thought that it was romantic. Some referred to him as "the desperate lover" and "the gatekeeper of his fiancée's dreams."

Anne Marie went to the room to chat with her mother, who usually went to bed by 8:30 p.m.

"Did you send the money to cousin Bernadette?" asked Méralie.

"Yes. Before I went to school this morning, I stopped by Island Sensation, the transfer place, and sent the money to Haiti. I think, by now, they should have received it."

"Thank you. We do not have much, but we cannot forget our relatives back there. Now, after that disaster, it is even worse. It is like a moral obligation. Who knows? Maybe it is for a time like this God placed us here. One good thing about the Haitian living in the diaspora, we don't forget our roots. We don't forget the ones left behind."

"By the way, Mommy," cut Anne Marie, "have you noticed any changes in Hyppolite lately?"

"He is perfectly fine," replied Méralie with a smile. "God has given me my son back. I am so grateful."

"I have been observing him lately," said Anne Marie. "I am talking about his good humor, the glow of his face, the light in his eyes. That doesn't have anything to do with driving a van. This is something more profound that show traces of love. Would he be in love without telling us?"

"I don't know," replied Méralie. "If a woman is the cause of this new attitude of my son, may God bless her, whoever she is."

Things could not get any better. Hyppolite was making payments on the car and helping in the house and, at the same time, was trying to save to go back to Haiti, which was his main objective. But from time to time, without expecting it, his mind went to Hellen.

This is not possible. I do not know how. I do not know when, but I must get this woman out of my mind.

Hellen, on her side, was getting more emotionally involved. She had been observing him. His seriousness and the way he was handling some situations and managing the business showed a man with great capacity and ability and a family-oriented citizen with manners and education. He had good eyes for administration, and most of all, he had the will to progress. She saw in him a person she could trust. To her, under this shell of "just come" with that heavy French accent, Hyppolite was a sharp, intelligent, and responsible man with a promising future. All he needed was a little polish and guidance in the right direction. So she had decided not to let go of him.

Although he picked her up every morning, she often called by lunchtime to speak to him. Lately it seemed that Hellen always had an urgent problem that required Hyppolite's presence. Every other day, for instance, she felt like eating Haitian food. Sometimes she just needed an aspirin for a terrible headache. In fact, there was always a good reason for her callings, but the real reason was obvious: she wanted to get his attention and keep him at her side the most time possible.

By the same token, Hyppolite was not annoyed at all with her musical, breathy voice. Although he was working hard to comply with his obligations, he had always found a way to come promptly to her rescue. Once, at her insistence, he even took her to his house at lunchtime to eat.

A Friday afternoon, he left the house at two o'clock as usual for work. He picked up the kids from school and dropped them to their homes. By 3:30 p.m., he picked up Hellen, who got off work early. On his way to Secaucus, he was stopped by two men who had an emergency to go to Manhattan. They begged for his help and offered to pay him the triple the trip. Since it was the beginning of the weekend, Hellen wanted to keep him company; by the end of the day, he would take her home.

The deal being sealed, the two men got in the car and sat in the back with an Igloo container, the kind you would take to a picnic. As the van was running, the traffic was slowing down. The cars were going as slow as ten miles an hour. And as usual, horns were blowing from everywhere; and behind the wheel, drivers did not stop cursing and complaining.

"Another day of traffic! How long are we going be stuck? Damn it! God, this is awful."

"Traffic on the major arteries. Traffic on the alternate lanes. Cars, vans, taxis, trucks, we are all stuck."

"What is going on? This is insane."

Coming from Hoboken, two blocks before turning into the Holland Tunnel, the van stopped; the traffic was at a complete standstill. Bumper to bumper and soul to soul, everyone was wondering what could possibly happen to cause such traffic jam. Suddenly the sirens of ambulances and fire trucks filling the air were loud enough to deafen any living being. Police in uniforms were running around all over the place. From two blocks away, you could see them pacing among the cars.

In the back of the van, the two men were going crazy. They were yelling at each other in a language that no one understood.

Then they moved upfront by the driver, yelling at Hyppolite, "Do something! Turn around! Let us go!"

In their hysteria, they were yelling just for yelling because the streets were completely packed: no car could move, not even one inch.

Hellen was still sitting at the passenger side, taking pictures of the traffic. As people were getting more upset, she turned the radio to 1010 Wins and advised the men to calm down and listen if they wanted to find out what was going on.

The news reported, "There is an incident at the Holland Tunnel. All inbound and outbound cars have been stopped. Traffic to the tunnel has been directed to Lincoln Tunnel, George Washington, and all outer borough bridges."

Not completely calmed, the men kept quiet for a while, hoping that soon the traffic would alleviate. While waiting, they saw two girls walking down Jersey Avenue. They were a block away. It seemed they were coming from the tunnel. Yelling, cursing, and throwing their arms up in the air, they were having a heated discussion. When they got close to the van, one of the men brought the window down and asked what was going on.

"I don't know what the hell is going on!" yelled one of the girls. "It is so confusing. There was a shooting at the tunnel. It seems they are looking for a fugitive. The police are on foot, patrolling the area inch by inch. You guys, if you think you are getting out of here soon, you better think again. It's crazy. Police with dogs are searching the cars and checking everybody inside before they let them move."

When the men heard the last sentence from the girls, their faces turned bright red.

"Uh-oh! Damn! Damn!" exclaimed one of them, tapping his feet, pulling his sleeves up, and shaking his long hair back.

Panicked, like animals trapped in cage, they were staring at each other like they were in a boxing ring. Suddenly they opened the door and fled like bullets coming out of a silencer. By the time Hyppolite realized that the van door was open, they already vanished and were long gone.

It was a cold and horrible day. Hyppolite finally got out of the traffic jam extremely late in the evening. He took Hellen home and drove back to Jersey City. He was so exhausted he did not bother having dinner. He kissed his mother good night and went to bed.

On Saturday morning, he got up early as usual hoping to have a better day. It was only when he got inside the van he realized that the men had left their Igloo container.

That was not a big deal, he thought.

While working, he would stop in the area he picked them up the day before and see if he could find them to return the container.

The day went on simply fine. It was cold, but it was a nice day. Traffic was good; business was not bad. Hyppolite made three trips to Hoboken trying to return the container; it was impossible. Getting in touch with these men was difficult; he did not know their name or anything about them. He only knew they were going to Manhattan, but he did not have an exact address. By the end of the day, he stopped by Hellen's house, bringing her flowers as a thank you for having supported him and keeping him company in that traffic mess that almost drove him to insanity.

Sunday was a serious holiday at Méralie's house. No one worked outside the home. For it was church and family day, a day to give thanks and rest. Although, in different occasions, he surprised himself thinking about Hellen, Hyppolite did not forget his goal: work as much as he could, save as much as he could, and go back to the island to take care of business. Since he was not as religious as the rest of the family, he would like to work at least half a day; but to please his mother, he stayed home. Meanwhile, his heart jumped at every ring of the phone, thinking Hellen was at the other end.

That Sunday morning, Tertulien drove the van to church with his mother, his sister, and his son, Joseph, who was spending the weekend with him. They had a beautiful service. Méralie came back home singing out loud the most joyful songs of the *Chants d'Esperance* book.

Still crazy over their new acquisition, all three brothers wanted to clean the van. Around 2:00 p.m., they grabbed their rags, their spray bottles, and took it to the back in the parking lot to do the job. Tertulien was still talking about the morning service: a preacher who had just come from Haiti gave a vibrant sermon that brought the whole congregation to tears.

While talking, the brothers took their time to dust and wipe any little spot; they went over the corners, all under the seats, etc. Once completed, the van was shiny inside and out. Although there was still snow on the ground, the tires were sprayed and polished.

"What about this?" said Tertulien, pointing at the Igloo container. "Who does it belong to?"

"Two men left it there last Friday evening," said Hyppolite. "I was about to drive them to Manhattan. The traffic was crazy. They get so upset they left without it. Yesterday I spent the whole day looking for them without any success."

"What's in it?" asked Esaie.

"I don't know what's in it. It's sealed with tape."

"You cannot keep a container in the van without knowing what it has inside," replied Esaie. "Now it is in your possession. If there are drugs inside, it is your responsibility. If you get stopped in the streets, the police won't believe that some men left it there."

Tertulien became nervous about the conversation. He grabbed a box cutter that was in the trunk, cut the tape, and opened the container. He then pulled out a package, quite heavy, all wrapped up in a plastic bag and secured with more tape. He cut the plastic open, and pieces of flesh fell out of the bag.

Visibly surprised, Esaie got closer, grabbed a twig on the ground, and moved the pieces around trying to find out what they were.

"These are organs, liver, kidneys, but I cannot tell from what."

"There is still some left," said Tertulien, who shook the bag.

Suddenly, to the horror of the men, a human hand fell out and rolled on the ground.

-8-

It's Not Easy

When the family finally made the purchased the van, they were full of hope that things would continue in the right direction. The brothers were excited; and Hyppolite, full of energy, was managing the business like a pro. Looking at her son in and out daily with such drive, Méralie's heart rejoiced. It was like waking up to a ray of sun on your window after a long, deep nightmare.

Everything was just fine when suddenly they opened their eyes to a crude reality. They found themselves in a challenging situation, at risk of getting caught with a bag of human body parts in their possession—a crime they did not commit.

When they made the shocking discovery, they were frozen on the spot. Standing in the middle of the yard looking at each other speechless, they lost control, as if they were suddenly transported to another planet.

Tertulien had the box cutter in one hand and a bloodstained plastic bag in the other. While his brother was rushing to put back the body parts in the container, he came back to his senses shaking, nervous, and upset.

"What is that? Is this a joke? What is going on? No! No! No!"

Yelling and kicking, he lost control, slipped on the snow, and hit his head on the bumper of the van. Esaie did not have time to pick up the package. He ran to Tertulien, holding his head, shaking and calling him. As he did not respond, Esaie asked Hyppolite for help. This one did not make one step forward. Like a body ripped of its soul, he stood there immobilized. Leaning on the van, he was staring straight ahead, breathing through his mouth without a sound.

Trapped between his brothers and the package scattered on the ground, Esaie did not know what to do. Not only was he worried for his brothers, but the parking lot belonged to the whole building. If anybody came out of his car and discovered the macabre spectacle, he did not know what would happen. As he bent on the ground over Tertulien, waves of fear, anger, and utter frustration overwhelmed him.

Meanwhile, Anne Marie was upstairs making sure Sunday dinner would be ready on time. Earlier, she had taken Joseph to the train station at Journal Square; he had to go back to his mother in Paterson. In the kitchen, she turned the stove on but could not do much. Her brothers were not answering their phones; she was not in peace. Like a premonition, she felt that something was wrong. From the kitchen window, she had a clear view of the street and the parking lot. Suddenly she dropped everything and went down. Without paying attention to anything else around her, she ran to Tertulien, who was still on the floor. She and Esaie put him in the van. She was drinking a bottle of water; she had to throw it on Tertulien's face to make him come back to himself.

"Thank you, Lord!" exclaimed Esaie, taking a deep breath. "I thought he had a heart attack."

Anne Marie was confused. She did not understand why Tertulien passed out, but the terrifying look on Esaie's face frightened her. Looking for an answer, she turned to Hyppolite, who had not completely recuperated but kept on repeating the same litany, "I can't believe this. I can't believe this. Damn! Oh, no! Damn!"

"What is going on? Why didn't you call 911?" yelled Anne Marie, panicked. "For God's sake, tell me what happened!"

As she became more and more nervous, Esaie tried to calm her down.

"Anne Marie, we cannot speak to you right now. Why don't you go ahead with Tertulien? We will meet upstairs."

"Please come with us," begged Anne Marie. "Tertulien is not feeling okay. You can help him up the stairs, just in case. He cares for everybody while he neglects himself. I am sure he didn't take his blood pressure pills this morning."

"Tertulien had the key to the van before he passed out," said Esaie. "We must find it and lock the van. We'll be right there."

Tertulien was hurting from the fall. Anne Marie had her arm around his shoulders while walking cautiously, going by the right side of the van.

"No!" screamed Esaie, who realized that his sister was about to discover the things on the ground. "Go to the other side!"

"You scared me to death. Why are you so nervous?" said Anne Marie.

"Sorry, we were cleaning the van. There is oil on the ground. Just go the other way," replied Esaie.

"I don't understand. You are acting weird. Something happened. I'll wait for you upstairs. I want to know what is going on."

Esaie did not pass out like Tertulien or react like Hyppolite, but his response to the discovery was not less dramatic. Trembling like a leaf, he cleaned up the ground, put the package back in the container, and sat inside the van with Hyppolite. Everything happened so fast he was in shock; he did not realize the gravity of the situation.

Now that he was trying to pull himself together, thousands of thoughts invaded his mind: *Who got killed? Is he someone we know? What about his loved ones? Are they looking for him? How did this package get inside the van? Where did it come from? What would we tell the police? What about Yanique, my fiancée? Would she believe that we are not criminals?*

Still shaking with emotion, Esaie looked around him with his hands over his head. The container was right there by his side; feeling noxious and scared, he jumped out of the van and turned to his brother.

"How the hell did this happen? Did you see when those guys were putting it in the van? Why didn't you ask what was in the container before you accepted it?"

"Do you think I let this happen on purpose?" replied Hyppolite. "If I had any suspicion, do you think I would have let them in? This is not my fault."

"Whose fault is it? Who was driving the van?"

They were still in the parking lot arguing when two neighbors entered the lot and parked right next to the van. One of them, a retired police officer, stood there for a while speaking to them and congratulating them for their new acquisition. As soon as the neighbor left, Hyppolite brought his brother back to their original conversation.

"Listen, man. Arguing will not solve the problem. If I could go back in time, I would have stayed in Haiti in the torment of that earthquake instead of bringing you such a problem. What is done is done. We cannot change the past. We are all upset, but we cannot let emotions cause us more trouble. We need to get rid of this thing as soon as possible. We won't be able to live in peace, knowing that it's in our possession or anywhere near us."

"We have been living in this neighborhood for so long. We are neither rich nor better than anyone else, but we have never had any problems. Now what? Now what is going to happen?"

Indeed, for the past twenty-five years, the family had been living in Jersey City, going through the routine of life with its ups and down like any citizen breathing under the sun. According to Méralie, most of the days were average: not too good and not too bad. Life went on day in and day out by the grace of the Lord. Difficulties came and went. The key is to never give up; if there is life, there is hope.

But since Hyppolite came to live with them, Méralie had a new vision of things with a new attitude. To her, everyone needed to give more thanks for what they had instead of complaining about what they did not accomplish because, after the tragedy of January 12, where so many people had been killed, any regular day aboveground was a good day.

The point is that emotion was running high in the family. Since that terrible earthquake, they were trying their best to make Hyppolite feel comfortable. Because he was directly involved, he was considered the most vulnerable. But the reality was none of them completely recuperated from the tragedy. Méralie did not want to accept that her nieces and nephew were gone. She would rather think that they were out of the country when the tragedy happened. The search for survival ended long ago, but deep inside, the whole family had hoped for a miracle. Not only they were mourning, but they were living with mixed feelings, swinging their moods from hope to anxiety. They thought some of their loved ones who disappeared were still alive somewhere and they needed help.

When Hyppolite started working with the van, the biggest challenge was to adapt to his new life and leave the past behind. At least that was everyone's wishes for him. His recuperation was a kind of consolation, bringing peace and serenity. But the discovery of the infamous "package" came to spoil everything. It was like a deep wound that started to heal slowly, and suddenly an accident caused it to reopen with more scaredness and more pain.

Since Friday evening the container was sitting inside the van, nobody paid any attention. Suddenly, on Sunday afternoon, it became an object of dread, throwing the three brothers under enough pressure to drive them insane.

It was difficult to understand how a split second could change their life or, more precisely, bring the whole family upside down. In other circumstances, the package would not cause so much trouble. They would immediately call the police, or it would be just a matter of acting cautiously and finding the right moment—and a spot—to dispose of it. The impact of that unfortunate discovery turned the situation to a bigger deal because the brothers currently were not psychologically ready for a surprise like that.

The container was kind of heavy, but Esaie could handle it. He took it out of the van and walked through the parking lot. Standing by the sidewalk, he buttoned his coat, looked on both sides of the streets, and tried to be as normal as he could. With a face good enough to mix with people going around the city, he walked out toward Jackson Avenue.

As usual, whether it is cold or not, Jersey City never missed its weekend happy strollers. Whether they are youngsters not willing to stay in the confinement of their homes, ladies walking their dogs, or couples in love who understand perfectly well that there is only one life to live, Sunday afternoons are always relaxing and happy.

Like an ambulant sherbet vendor out of ice, Esaie held the container tight under his arm and was going down Gifford Avenue with determination. The idea was to dispose of it in the first vacant lot he found. This sounded like a plan; but he forgot that Takeema, the lady across the street, had him on a short leash. Since she was not welcome in his house, she always stayed outside the building, monitoring his every move. For some reason, she was obsessed with him, and she was not about to let go.

All stressed out, Esaie was walking up Gifford Avenue quietly but as fast as he could with the hope to soon free his hands. Just before turning onto Jackson Avenue, he noticed that somebody was running after him.

"I have been calling you since you walked out of the parking lot. Where are you going? Why do you have this Igloo container? Why are you not driving? Let me help you."

Nervous and scared, Esaie kept on walking without paying attention to Takeema, who did not give up.

"I don't understand you anymore. You used to be so attentive, so gentle. You have changed. Why this angry face? Why are you so weird, so nervous? What's wrong?"

"This face is the only one that I have. I am not in the mood," said Esaie. "I told you many times I have someone in my life. I do not want to be bothered. Please leave me alone."

"Why are you so mean to me? I still love you."

"Stop it!" yelled Esaie in a rush. "I don't want to talk to you, not now, not ever. It's over!"

Takeema spent the whole afternoon following him, asking for money for cigarettes and trying to convince him to speak to her. Esaie became more and more frustrated. His whole life was in jeopardy walking with that package in the streets. He could not get rid of Takeema, and because of her, he could not get rid of the package that felt heavier at every step.

At the corner of Fairmont and Monticello Avenue, he finally put the container down; and with a mounting feeling of rage, he looked straight at the woman who would not stop getting on his nerves. Only one thought came to his mind: he would like to launch his fist right into her big mouth that did not stop talking and knock her down right there. But as people were going by, he changed his mind. He shook his head, picked up the container, and went back home with Takeema following him up to the gate.

Hyppolite was waiting at the parking lot. Esaie came back and put the Igloo container down.

"Why didn't you leave it somewhere? What made you change your mind?"

Esaie did not hear his brother who was speaking to him. Full of fury, he was cursing and kicking the container.

"Calm down!" yelled Hyppolite, who grabbed him by the back, immobilizing him. "This parking lot is an open space. People are looking at you through their windows. Do you want them to come down and find out what is going on? Do you want them to call the police? Is that what you want? Damn, man! We cannot let this situation drive us crazy!"

"I had the opportunity to take care of it," said Esaie. "I tried to drop it, but Takeema was like my shadow, following me step-by-step, breathing down my neck! She did not give me any chance."

Standing in the parking lot, the two brothers were helpless. Esaie did not want to put the container back inside the van. He looked in all directions, trying to find a place to hide it until a better opportunity come up; he could not even find a hole or a discreet corner.

The afternoon was coming to an end. Slowly the early evening darkness brought along snow flurries that embraced the whole city. The light flakes dusted down over the parking lot, covering the cars. Some people who were out rushed back home before it became heavier. Sitting inside the van thinking, Esaie checked the time.

"What do I do now? The snow came unexpectedly. Is it a harbinger, a way out? Anyway, 6:30 p.m. is still early, too early to make another move."

Like convicted criminals, the two brothers left the parking lot silently, side by side but as tense as they could be. In the apartment, Esaie could not stand still, pacing the floor with his heart beating like a drum. He was thinking and thinking, but no idea came to his mind. He took a deep breath and turned toward his brothers, who were just sitting in the living room, their hands holding their pale faces with a desperate demeanor. Not knowing what to say or to do, he moved away from them and went to the bathroom. He turned the water on to wash his hands and refresh his face. Looking at the mirror, Esaie lamented with indignation.

Life is weird. It is the biggest con of all. Sometimes it promises you great things, and to better accommodate your expectations, it even gives a glimpse of what can be or accomplished. With the hope for a better tomorrow, you spend the whole time reinventing yourself with the implicit purpose of granting success or that peace of mind so long striving for. And just when you think you are at the end of the tunnel, you come face-to-face with the cruel reality. You have invested all your hope in an illusion.

Takeema is a curse. She is stalking me so much that I cannot do anything. She is the reason why we still have this package. Now, not only Hyppolite is implicated, but we are also accomplices in this mess.

-9-

Take Life as It Comes

Meanwhile, Méralie was waiting with the good humor she had conserved since the morning service; dinner would soon be served. As she stood by the kitchen window, moist by the steamy vapor of the pots, her biggest gratification was to have the whole family together in a relaxing mood on Sunday. During the week, everybody was running on different schedule. As a typical Haitian woman, she did not have to chase after anybody to eat. The delicious aroma of her kitchen was stimulation to the appetite, an invitation to the table. The Sunday menu did not disappoint: the famous chicken cooked in spicy gravy, rice and kidney beans, and fried plantain and watercress and sliced tomatoes as salad and the delicious sweet potato bread as desert.

She had waited for a while, and since nobody came in, she got up to tell them dinner was overdue. But as soon as she got to the hallway, she sensed that something was wrong. The look on the boys' face said it all. She stopped a minute and went back to the kitchen.

"I have a bad premonition," she told Anne Marie. "Why are they so pale, so nervous? What is going on?"

"It's cold. Let me bring them coffee," said Anne Marie, already nervous. "Stay here. I will find out what's going on."

Still standing in the bathroom with the water running, Esaie was thinking that either Hyppolite or Tertulien needed to take care of the package. Takeema, that woman across the street, was too much of a risk. When he came out to join his brothers, the look in their eyes, as if they were ready to pass judgment, stopped him in his tracks. He did not even sit down; his frustration soon turned to anger.

"What is going on?" he said. "What the hell are you thinking? Why are you looking at me like that?"

"We are not thinking about anything," replied Tertulien, outraged. "We just don't understand your foolishness. In a horrific situation like this, we can even go to jail, I do not know how far your cynicism would go. Where did you find the guts walking in the streets with Takeema like two teenagers in love instead of taking care of that thing?"

"What you don't understand," yelled Esaie, "is that it would be too much of a risk getting into a fight with her, using force to push her away, while I was in the streets carrying evidence of a crime!"

"What?" yelled Anne Marie, who let go of the coffee tray she was bringing to them.

Esaie's statement echoed in Anne Marie's ears and hit like a sledgehammer. Looking at her brothers and trembling with fear, she lost her balance. Tertulien and Hyppolite jumped up in their seats, grabbed her, and sat her down by their side while trying to reason with her. Esaie himself did not know when he let the statement out. Surprised and embarrassed, he did not know how to fix the situation. In a moment of desperation, he threw a punch at the wall that left a hole in Méralie's living room.

"Nobody told me exactly what was going on," whispered Anne Marie, trembling. "I only know from Tertulien that something very grave had shocked all three of you. But I never thought you were talking about crime. Oh my God! Oh my God! Mommy won't avoid such deception when she finds out that she has raised criminals."

Tertulien's and Hyppolite's words tumbled one on top of the other. They were going around the subject without a good explanation and without any sense. Meanwhile, dinner was getting cold. Since no one came forward, Méralie went back to the living room calling them to the table; but once again, the picture she got was not to boost anyone's appetite. Anne Marie, all trembling, was crying with a livid face. Hyppolite was tapping his feet incessantly, but his eyes clearly revealed the emptiness of his mind. The tension was enough to make anybody crazy inside the house. Méralie tried to speak to them; this time, even Anne Marie was mute. Since nobody was willing to talk, thousands of negative thoughts flew through her mind. She was a guide, the pillar that kept the family together, as a mother who knew each one of her children. She went to her room with her blood pressure skyrocketing.

By 8:00 p.m., Mohammad rang the bell.

"I'm sorry to come at this time, but I have been calling all afternoon, and no one answered the phone. I just want to check what is going on. Are you okay?"

"Yes, I am all right," said Anne Marie, hesitating. "I can't talk too much now. I have a headache. I may be catching a cold."

"This is not like you, Annie," said Mohammad. "You look nervous and sad. Please do not hide things from me. If we are together, we are supposed to support each other in good and bad times. I am your friend. I love you. We are in a relationship. If something is wrong, you need to tell me. The solution might be right here, and you do not know it. I'm here to help, whatever it is."

Thinking her boyfriend might be supportive, Anne Marie told him what she knew and explained the actual situation of tension she and her brothers were living in.

Mohammad went across the street and stood on the sidewalk, looking at the building. *What could be so grave to shock those three guys to the point they were out of control? Evidence of crime! Who is the victim? These cowards do not have the guts to kill anybody unless an accident. I am sure the crime they are talking about has to do with drug or money. But why didn't they want Anne Marie to walk by the right side of the van?*

As an opportunist ready to jump on any good occasion that came across, Mohammad would not let this pass by. With the feeling that something big was coming up, he was alert. He did not move from the block. He would like to find something, anything, to use against them—any proof of wrongdoing that would give him the opportunity to challenge them and, if necessary, nail them. But no matter what, Anne Marie was in the middle. He had to find a way to get to them without touching her. As he was still standing across the street, watching and thinking, an idea enlightened his mind, with a malicious smile on his face.

I cannot yet pinpoint exactly what they did, but whatever it is, this is a golden opportunity to cut a deal, a pact of silence with them. They accept my relationship with their sister, and I will keep my mouth shut. I am sick and tired of standing outside, waiting for Anne Marie to come out.

As he was there lost in his crazy thoughts, Takeema joined him; they went to the liquor store, got a quart of Bacardi, and started a conversation.

Esaie had been sitting by the kitchen window. His watch marked exactly 9:00 p.m.; it was still early. Like a watchdog, he was on alert, always checking the parking lot and the front gate. The package could not stay in the van any longer.

It was not as easy as he thought to get rid of it earlier. Besides Takeema's indiscretion, Sunday afternoon was not the best time to take care of a matter like that. People living in the Bergen area of Jersey City do not rest. They care very much for their walk; they are not too much on observing other people and gossiping, but they are aware of public safety. Anyone who looks suspicious or any unattended package will get their attention in a heartbeat.

Esaie waited until everything was calm. By 11:00 p.m., he grabbed his key and snuck out of the house. He did not want to call his brothers. After the ordeal of the afternoon, they were still too emotional to count on them. It was cold; all at once, the snowflakes stopped, leaving the streets quiet and deserted. At the first opportunity, he would drop the package along with the container somewhere—case closed. He went silently to the parking lot, got the container out of the van, put it in the trunk of his car, and left without knowing that Mohammad was across the street smoking and drinking with Takeema and they had decided to follow him.

From Gifford Avenue, Esaie turned to Kennedy Boulevard, drove only two blocks, and had to stop at Communipaw Avenue. The streets ahead were blocked and completely lit up with flashing lights. While trying to turn around, an officer walked over to him and touched his window with a baton.

Just seeing the officer, he got hot and cold simultaneously. His mouth and throat became dry. His whole body was shaking, and he could barely talk. Sitting behind the wheel, he breathed deeply, tried to compose himself, and rolled down his window.

"Yes, Officer?"

"Where are you heading?" asked the policeman, who projected a flashlight on his face while checking the back seat.

"Not far. I'm going to Clendenny Avenue."

Kennedy Boulevard was being closed for police activity; so he detoured to West Side Avenue, drove a quarter mile, and stopped for a minute. He was so close to getting busted with the package in his car. But he came out to take care of that thing. One way or the other, it must go; he just needed to be careful. He turned the key in the ignition and put his signal on, and just when he was about to drive off, Takeema opened the door and sat on the passenger side.

"Please! I need a ride back home," she begged. It's cold. I have been waiting so long for a bus that I cannot stand on my feet any longer."

Esaie got out, opened the passenger door, and asked Takeema to vacate the car. Although he stood there holding the car door open, waiting for her to leave, she did not move from her seat. Furious, Esaie grabbed her shirt to pull her out of the car.

As she started yelling, crying, begging, and making a spectacle, a couple who was walking by advised him, "Just go home with your wife and take care of whatever business with her. Otherwise, both of you could get arrested for being a public nuisance!"

Meanwhile, police cars with sirens and flashing lights were going around all over. No one knew what was going on. Esaie did not insist. Sweating with fear and rage, he got in the car and drove back home. Before entering the parking lot, he grabbed Takeema by her shoulder and pushed her away.

"You're hurting me!"

"This is the last time you stalk me like this. You won't be so lucky next time."

Esaie ran up the stairs two steps at a time and took refuge in his room, out of breath, like he was being chased by a pit bull. The truth is the package was becoming a hot potato, difficult to get rid of.

The rest of the evening was just pure torture. The night seemed unending. Tormented like demons in hell, the brothers could not close their eyes; they spent agonizing hours, reliving the outrageous event of the day repeatedly. The biggest question was why. Why would someone hate them to the point of trying to frame them like this? Hyppolite did not like to speak out when a problem showed up. But his mind did not stop running. As he sat on the bed, a sick and painful memory rushed into his mind, sneaking up on his thoughts like a mugger. He shook his head.

"I can't take this anymore," he whispered.

Suddenly he stood up, grabbed his coat, and was heading to the door when Tertulien stopped him.

"Let me go!" said Hyppolite, pushing his brother aside. "I need a drink. This package is my responsibility. No matter what happens to me, I do not care. I am going out to take care of it. I should have known better than to take these guys in the van. It seems that calamities are following me wherever I go. I shouldn't bring you such problems."

"Don't blame yourself," said Esaie. "The van is not equipped with a bad-guy detector that would go off when criminals get in. You do not know who is good, who is bad. Besides, the streets are invaded with police cars. I do not know what is going on, but it is too risky to go out now. Have faith. We will get out of this."

"It's not easy to relive the same macabre scenario repeatedly," said Hyppolite, crashing down on a chair.

"What are you talking about?"

"After the unfortunate tragedy in January, I spent weeks in torment. I witnessed the most horrific things I have ever seen. That 7.0-magnitude earthquake crushed thousands of structures. The devastated city of Port-au-Prince was worse than a war zone. Death hovered over it like a vulture.

"Wherever you turned, there were dead bodies. Everywhere you walked, you were stepping on body parts. From schools and shacks to the National Palace and the local UN headquarters. Bodies of tiny children were piled next to schools. Corpses of women lay on the streets with stunned expressions frozen on their faces. Bodies of men were covered with plastic tarps or cotton sheets.

"So many buildings have been destroyed or made uninhabitable and so many services were disrupted. All the roads were blocked. They could not clean up right away. With a broken heart, I saw people dying without assistance. I saw kids lying on the floor missing parts of their body. I could not sleep. Every time I closed my eyes, the whole tragedy flashed back in front of me. I was going crazy.

"When I finally got here, I started working with this van, trying to breathe and forget. The promise of a new day started to smile at me. I felt relief. I thought I saw a light, but it was only a mirage in the desert. It was just a blurry, blind, and distractive perception. I will never get rid of my bad luck. The proof is that package with body parts landing in *my* van. From all those taxis, buses, and vans going around the city, those bandits had chosen my van to carry out their bad deed. This is a nightmare that brought me back to the episode of horror, the torturing and horrifying moments I have already lived. Only this time in the equation, I look more like a suspect than a victim."

Esaie and Tertulien were listening to Hyppolite with attention. For the first time, he finally spilled his heart. He talked about the tragedy that had affected him so much. They knew nobody could go through so much and come out completely unaffected, but to them, this was a good sign to recovery.

By 2:00 a.m., Hyppolite and Tertulien finally fell asleep. Esaie did not stop tossing and turning. Lying on his back in the dark of the room with his eyes wide open, he was tormented. This thing was a danger that jeopardized the whole family. Since he was the one representing them when it came to deal with the outside, he felt like he had more responsibility than the others in this matter. One more time, he snuck out of the house and went back to his car.

This time, it seemed luck was in Esaie's favor. The whole city seemed to be sleeping. There was not a sound or a soul; not even Takeema was there. The silence was rested so well and so deep over the city that, if you blew a horn hard enough in Journal Square, people would have heard it in the Bergen area. From Gifford Avenue, he took Communipaw straight down, crossing Westside Avenue and Route 440 until Nguyen and Carson Bridge. Finally, finally, he will be able to get rid of this torment. He stopped for a minute, just the time to get out of the car; grabbed the container; and threw it over the bridge. Suddenly a vehicle coming out of nowhere stopped right behind him with the high beam on.

"What's going on here?" yelled a man at the passenger side. "I'm calling the police. Whatever you have in that container, either you eat it, smoke it, or you turn yourself in. And do not you dare speed away. You can run, but you cannot hide. We will be on your tail until we nail you to the ground."

Esaie snapped! Since the container was found inside the van, he was scared and frustrated. At the same time, he was trying to be strong to support his brothers. But this was the last drop to overflow the vase. Standing on top of that bridge with the light blinding him and with the ever-increasing cold wind passing through his body, he felt like a screen door. He turned his head up as if he wanted to call upon the Lord, but the gray and empty sky seemed like it was coming down on him. He looked down the empty space; the river was not anything else but an icy dark blanket. Esaie was trembling like a mouse caught in a glue trap. He did not understand where that car suddenly came from, why these men were following him, or how much they knew.

Instantly all his thoughts dissolved and were replaced by a blind, mind-numbing fear. His best way out would be taking a leap of resignation, opting for a free fall and, once and for all, terminating this torture. But in a split second, one last thought rushed into his mind. He made a step back, jumped instead into his car, and took off. On the verge of a nervous breakdown, he did not pay attention to the road signs and to the people behind him or even know where he was going. He did not know how long he drove, but when he finally realized his tank was empty, he was on the road to Trenton. He managed to get to a gas station to no avail. He had to wait; at that time of night, all the stations were closed.

Meanwhile, Tertulien and Hyppolite were going crazy. They did not notice when Esaie left the house; they had been waiting for more than two hours. They kept quiet to not disturb their mother and sister, but they were worried sick. Any sound of a car passing by in the streets and any sound of footsteps going up the stairs caught their attention. Even the barking of a dog made their heart jump. From time to time, they ran to the window thinking Esaie was coming.

It was seven thirty-five the next morning when Esaie finally made it back home. All dirty, wrinkled, and tired, he looked like a reject from an ammunition explosion. He locked himself in his room and did not come out until his sister took Méralie to her doctor's appointment.

"What happened to you?" asked his brothers, still nervous. "You spent the rest of the night out. Now you look like hell. What more could have happened?"

It seems that Esaie had reached his breaking point. As he stood with his hands in his pocket, tears rolled down his cheeks.

"We are in a very delicate situation. I cannot take it anymore. I am tired. I think we are being framed. Since we did not do anything wrong, we need to call the police because it will be much worse if we get caught with that thing in our possession."

Tertulien was not too comfortable with the idea. "Hyppolite did not know what was in that package. The passengers fled and left it on purpose in the van. Now it is too late to bring this matter to the police's attention because that would cause more problems. It would take time, energy, and a lawyer that we will not be able to afford to prove our innocence. We must go farther out, away from the city— to Pennsylvania, for instance—and dispose of it along the way."

Esaie slammed the palm of his hand against his forehead with a gesture of impatience. "You do not understand! The situation is worse than you think. We are being framed! Someone has been following us! They want to drive us crazy."

"This is not possible that we are trapped like that," said Tertulien, frightened. "We just needed to work. We are fighting for survival, not anything else. Oh my God! Who is doing this to us? Why?"

"This is a difficult situation," said Hyppolite. "For all of us, it is not easy. But please try to calm down. We need to find a solution as soon as possible. Thank God it's not hot out there. Otherwise, I don't know what we would do."

"It seems we will not get out of this. In Jersey City, I already tried twice. It was impossible get rid of it. Now I am sure whoever wants to get us in trouble is out there watching us closely."

As they were debating the situation, somebody rang the bell. Mohammad, with his hands in his pockets, walked slowly and safely and settled down in the living room, his feet lying on the table.

"What do you want?" asked Tertulien. "Anne Marie is not here."

In response, he leaned back with an air of quiet majesty, drew a cigar from his pocket, and began to smoke.

"First of all," said Esaie, "in this house, nobody smokes. Secondly you do not have any right to enter people's houses like this without saying even good morning and put your dirty feet on the table. You need to leave, and please do not come back."

Mohammad became more belligerent.

"I'm waiting for her," responded Mohammad arrogantly. "Is there a problem with that? You cannot fool me. Do you think going out in the streets groomed and dressed like a nineteenth-century man will make you a gentleman? Do you think acting like a serious citizen will reverse the situation? I know who you all are. If you think you can throw the rock and hide your hands, you have another thought coming."

"What are you insinuating?" said Esaie, nervous.

"Instead of treating me like I am less than nothing, why do not we try to live in peace? I love your sister. Believe me, it is not a joke. I am serious, and I want to marry her. I know a lot of things about you guys. You accept me as part of the family, and everything will be okay."

Esaie, who was already bitter and frustrated for all that happened the night before, could not control his impulses any longer. He got up from his seat, and with a fury he never felt before, he was ready to shut him up with his bare hands.

"Hey! Hey!" yelled Mohammad, showing the palm of his hand raised up like a stop sign. "Do not you dare touch me, or I call 911 right away. Be careful. You are walking on thin ice here. I will not hesitate to tell them you have something to hide. Now, if you can afford a police investigation, it is up to you."

"This man is drunk," said Tertulien, who had time to stop Esaie. "Don't let his comments darken your day more than it already has."

Anne Marie was still at the clinic with Méralie, but she was too tense to wait quietly. Every time she remembered the weird behavior of her brothers, emotions shocked her heart. As for Esaie's explosive statement, with every sigh, the echo of the words rushed into vibrations in her mind. She felt trapped; she did not know what to think. Suddenly she walked out and went back home, deciding to have a serious conversation with her brothers. This time, whether they liked it or not, they would have to put all the cards on the table.

She was coming up the stairs when she heard noises coming from her apartment like people were arguing. She rushed in and opened the door to find Mohammad in the middle of an argument.

"You are calling me drunk. Who do you think you are? You and your people came to America with your tail between your legs, like dogs running away from trouble. God knows from what kind of dirty business! Before you could even speak a word of English, you were already too much. As soon as you got a job, you swelled like a frog. Now, Jersey City is not enough for you. You think that you are a big shot, better than everybody."

"For your information," said Esaie, "this is America! It is a free country, a country of opportunity. You can be all you want to be if you abide by the law. If you are messing up your life, it is your business! If we choose to excel, you are not going to stop us. Thank God this is America!"

"Get out of here!" said Hyppolite threateningly. "Do not you dare come back."

"You, wise guy, you better run while you can! You better hurry up and go back to where you came from before it is too late. You do not know what I have in store for you. Do not think you will get away with it. I will be after you step-by-step. I will be watching."

"Get away with what?" said Anne Marie, surprised and nervous. "Mohammad, what is going on? Why are you yelling so much?"

"Nothing, darling," he said, giving her a kiss. "I will see you later." Mohammad was already at the door leaving. He turned around to say a last word to the men, "You think I'm not good enough for your sister, right? You think you are better than me. I will not let you break the law and still go around Jersey City acting like respectable people."

Anne Marie was so confused and ashamed that she could not face her brothers, who were asking for an explanation. They knew Mohammad was not a good man, but why did he suddenly become so arrogant? Why so abusive? How much did he know? Anne Marie broke in tears.

"I am sorry. I am so sorry. He promised to help. I thought he would be a support for us. I told him we were having problems. Everybody was nervous in the house. This is something that has to do with the van."

"Mohammad won't hesitate to bring the police to search the van," said Hyppolite, hands over his head.

"I won't let him do that. I will speak to him," said Anne Marie.

"Don't you dare!" yelled Esaie. "I hope you now understand that Mohammad is not a man for you. He does not love you because a man who really loves a woman does not make her family his enemies, at least not before he gets married. Besides, love does not threaten. Love does not blackmail, and love does not take advantage of any situation to hurt. You better stay away from this bastard for your own good."

Meanwhile, all the phones in the house were ringing off the hook. Anne Marie did not pick up just in case Mohammad was calling. The brothers were too busy smashing their head to find a way out; they did not have time to talk on the phone.

Hyppolite could not stand this nervous atmosphere for one more minute. Sitting in his room, he was staring at his cell that kept on ringing. He finally put his jacket on, left the phone on the bed, and walked out the door.

By 2:00 p.m., Méralie came back alone from the doctor. As she opened the door, her heart jumped into her throat; the house was in total chaos. It was like a ticking bomb, ready to explode. Tertulien was sitting in the kitchen with his head leaning on the table. Esaie was still pacing the floor like a tiger. Anne Marie had her eyes completely red from crying, and when it came to Hyppolite, he was nowhere to be found.

Standing in the living room, she shook her head with anxiety. *This is getting out of hand. This is depressing. It seems that a mysterious disaster has raged through my children and left them in complete desolation. Today is Monday. Nobody went to work. The van is sitting in the middle of the yard without Hyppolite. The worst part of it is nobody is speaking. I do not know what is going on.*

Méralie went to her room, closed the door, and kneeled in front of her bed to pray. In any difficult situation, she was in the habit of looking for guidance from a higher power before doing anything. Since the death of her husband, she had turned down all opportunities to have another man. "God will provide" was the words she never stopped saying.

Esaie and Tertulien, knowing Méralie was going to ask questions they would not want to answer, took advantage that their mother went to her room to get out of the house. The two men went through the neighborhood searching for Hyppolite, but just a simple look at them would tell something was wrong. Esaie, who usually had a pleasant look on his face and a twinkle in his eyes, was going around with a desperate demeanor and grimacing expression on his face. You would think he had just been pulled out from under those building destroyed by the earthquake.

No one saw Hyppolite in the neighborhood. As expected, Takeema, the lady across the street, did not take time to show up. She quickly offered her help and wanted to accompany them in their search. Esaie categorically refused.

"Please, madame, leave me alone. I already have enough in my mind. Stay away from me, or I will file a restraining order against you."

From Gifford Avenue, going from street to street, they finally found Hyppolite at Journal Square standing at the corner of Sip and Bergen Avenue with a pack of cigarettes in his hand. The three brothers went across the street to a restaurant, ordered a coffee, and sat down to talk.

"This is profoundly serious," said Esaie. "All of us need to try on our part to get out of this trouble. Mommy is very perceptive. She knows something bad is going on. She is getting nervous. She is asking questions, and we do not want her to get sick. You, Hyppolite, I am not asking you to be happy. I am not asking you to be joyful or content. This is an inward feeling of satisfaction that none of us can afford presently. Besides, they do not sell it at the store, but you need to learn to control yourself. Do not make the problem worse. You cannot just go out the door without saying a word. Now you are standing in the street, doing nothing with a pack of cigarettes in your hands. You're a grown man. You can do whatever you want, but if you've never smoked before, now is not the best time to start."

"Our brother is right," continued Tertulien. "We need to think and stick together. We don't know if Mohammad has a connection with the men who left the container inside the van, but we know that he is trying to get us in trouble."

"By the way," said Esaie, "you had left your cell phone in the house. Here it is. The van did not go out today. Customers continue to call. Please tell them we are fixing a problem. It will be back out as soon as possible."

"Another reason that we need to hurry up with this matter. The van needs to go back in the streets. Otherwise, we won't be able to keep up the monthly payments."

Meanwhile, in the house, things were not too quiet. Méralie came out of her room more decided than ever; she asked to speak with everybody. The boys being out, she went right to the point with Anne Marie.

"Since yesterday afternoon, this house is upside down. I have been trying to find out, but nobody wants to talk. Now I am asking you the same question. What is going on? And please do not tell me nothing is going on because I am not an idiot. If any of you did something wrong, I want to know about it. I am tired of your mouths being closed while your frightened faces are shouting trouble."

Anne Marie remembered what happened with Mohammad. She did not want to make the same mistake and unveil the whole truth to her mother.

"Popo had a little problem the other day while working. He almost got to an accident, but it was not bad. He made an agreement with the other driver to fix it. Police did not get involved. He also needs to fix something in the van. You know how much of a perfectionist he is. That is why he is affected more than he should be, but it is not a big deal. Esaie and Tertulien are with him. I suggest that you do not ask them any questions for now. I am sure, when they fix the problem completely, they will tell you.

"The biggest problem we had yesterday was Mohammad. He became very arrogant and aggressive. He came to the house when you were at the doctor's office. He almost got into a fight with my brothers."

"Mohammad is mysterious. You, as a child of God, should not have anything to do with him unless telling him about the Gospel of Christ. From what I could observe, since he has been coming to the house, he is a passive man. People do not suddenly become violent overnight for no apparent reason unless if he is using illegal drugs. I don't understand him."

"I never saw him using drugs or alcohol," said Anne Marie, annoyed by the conversation. "He just doesn't get along with my brothers."

"You need to reconsider your position with that man. If a man does not get along with your family, you need to be careful. In any situation, you need to be careful of who you are choosing as friends. Your friends will either add to your happiness or undermine it. Their attitudes and conversations are bound to affect your outlook on life. If Mohammad is acting like that now, what would happen if one day you two got married? It would be hell. Some people are just poison. You don't always know it, but when you finally find out, you need to cut them out of your life before it is too late."

-10-

What's New?

"Love is a God-given gift to humanity," used to say Anne Marie while talking to her friend Raquel. "Allow it to grow, and whether you are rich or poor, your life will bloom like a flower opening to the morning sun. Like the heart keeps the body going, love makes life worth living."

Although the family never approved of her relationship with Mohammad, she was happy, living a dream, and thinking he was the best man on earth. It had been six months since she met him at a social event at Liberty Park. From the first moment their eyes met, they were attracted to each other; it was like love at first sight. Mohammad was kind, attentive, and friendly with a nice sense of humor. He was somehow mysterious yet charming with a contagious smile; he took her high as a kite. To her, he was everything she ever hoped for and dreamed for; she felt loved.

But since the latest event that happened at the house, she was sad and tormented. She did not know exactly what was going on with her brothers, but she was worried even more about her relationship with Mohammad. When did he change so much?

As she sat in the kitchen, the family's advice kept on flashing back like a bad dream.

Be selective about people you allow in your life. You have greatness in you. You have potential.

Your seed can set a new standard for yourself and your family. You can break a generation of curse.

Do not let yourself be contaminated. This man is not the man for you.

Do not let people's negativity choke out your joy, your faith, and your victory.

The sound of these words went through her heart like a knife, but what hurt the most was that she was conscious of the fact that the family might have been right.

She could not forget coming home and finding Mohammad making a scene and threatening her brothers. She never saw him so crude and offensive.

Why was he so aggressive? Why was he trying to accuse them? Why was he threatening them?

So many questions were running through her mind with no answers. She went to her room and spent the rest of the afternoon crying.

By 5:30 p.m., Mohammad came to the door asking for her. She did not come out. Although he insisted on seeing her to explain the scene she witnessed, she refused to speak to him. Overwhelmed by the situation, Anne Marie did not know what to do.

Sitting in her room, giving free rein to her thoughts, she murmured, "There are times in life when you must make difficult choices, and there are times when it seems you don't have any choice at all. The best thing to do is cut him off completely. Yes! This is the right decision.

"But can you command your heart? Can you order it to stop loving? Can you cut someone out of your life like you cut your fingernails? How do you say goodbye to someone you cannot live without?

"Who is Mohammad? Do I really know him? When did he become so mean? Why?"

Between thinking and crying, she thought she was going crazy.

Mohammad had always been a tough guy. He was both a book- and street-smart type of guy who never turned down good opportunities. Raised by a mother who died too young from drug addiction, he went from foster home to foster home during his adolescence. All of this made him spiteful and self-conscious. Although he had difficult times in his young age, he was an intelligent boy, doing well in school; but also he had learned a lot from the streets. He had had many relations with other women, but never did he mix business with pleasure.

When he met Anne Marie, he approached her just because of her pretty face. But as time passed, he let his guard down. Emotions got the better of him; he fell in love. For this reason, he had tried very hard to control his impulses, and all that time, he was trying to convince Anne Marie to move with him. But patience was not his virtue; the rejection of the family infuriated him. As soon as he knew the brothers were in trouble, the opportunist in him could not help trying to frame them and get even. He jumped on the occasion to teach them a lesson.

Along with a couple of friends he hired and with Takeema's help, he was to watch them closely and had succeeded in stopping them from getting rid of whatever they had in their car. The plan was to blackmail and weaken them until they quit their pride—that attitude of honest gentlemen they were claiming. But somehow something went wrong. Mohammad did not expect Anne Marie to leave her mother alone at the clinic only to find him threatening her family in their own house. For drinking a bit more than he should, he went overboard and let his frustration out too soon; he blew it. Afraid that Anne Marie did not want to see him anymore, he went across the street scratching his head and hoping that, sometime that evening, she would come out and he would have a chance to speak with her.

The brothers were walking home from Journal Square, where they picked up Hyppolite. Tertulien was on the phone with Joseph, who alleged that his mother's boyfriend punched him in the face and this was not the first time the man mistreated him.

Since Hyppolite did not answer his phone, Esaie stopped a minute to listen to the messages in case a client called for car service. One of the messages was from Hellen.

"Hyppolite, I have been calling you since yesterday. You did not answer your phone. To me, it has been an eternity. It is too much of a strain, sitting in the house all day, hoping that you would stop by. I have not moved away from my window, craning my nose and eyes to see if you are coming up the street. You will never know how big and devastating is the love I have for you. But I want to tell you that, if you do not want to speak to me, I understand. Love is magic and beautiful when it is natural. But it is so capricious that you cannot force it. I hope that you are okay. Take care of yourself. Bye."

Mohammad and Takeema were sitting across the street when the men arrived in front of their building. She was about to approach Esaie when Mohammad stopped her.

"Why are you so jumpy? Don't you see all three are together? I do not want them to know that I am still around. This morning, I cursed out all three of them. I am trying to find out the reason they are acting so weird."

"Aren't you afraid that they will beat you up?"

"These men, the only thing they have is a stupid and unjustified pride," said Mohammad. "That Christian widow they have for mother shadowed them too much in her skirt. They have become more delicate than girls coming out of a convent. They are frightened by anything. They didn't have a role model, a father who would teach them how to be men."

"What are you saying?" replied Takeema. "Esaie is a real man. There is nothing shy or girly about him."

"If you were a good observer," said Mohammad, smiling, "you would know behavior is sometimes more revealing than language. Those dudes are a bunch of idiots. They should not get into any business they cannot handle. Their so-called good education will be their damnation."

"What business?" questioned Takeema with a more serious tone. "You know well what is going on, don't you? You do not want to tell me. Esaie has been acting weird since yesterday. He is nervous and suspicious of something. I want to know his weakness. That is the only way he will come back to me. Yesterday afternoon, he walked all around the city carrying an Igloo container. He did not stop anywhere to talk to anyone. I know he is not crazy. Please help me find out what is wrong with him."

Mohammad's face suddenly lighted with a funny smile; an idea came to his mind.

"Bingo!" he cried. "The Igloo!"

"What is going on? Are you going to help me?" asked Takeema, desperate.

"I do not waste my precious time interfering in stupid relations between men and women," said Mohammad. "These futilities or banalities do not interest me. I have serious business to take care. Time is money."

Mohammad pulled out his cell phone, texting without paying more attention to Takeema, who was looking at him walking away. She was puzzled; the expression of his face did not convince her. She was certain that Mohammad knew more than what he was saying. She discreetly followed him to the corner of Communipaw Avenue, where he stopped to speak with two friends who were waiting for him. Hiding behind a pole, she was listening to their conversation.

"We followed Esaie until the bridge last night," said one of the men. "We stopped him from getting something out of his car. We could not continue after him because that dude is crazy. He took off as if he were driving straight to hell. I'm surprised he is still alive."

"This dude is suddenly acting weird," said Mohammad, thinking out loud. "Something is going on with that Igloo container."

"They must be transporting some goods out there," said one of the friends. "What do we do now?"

"It is very important they mess up," said Mohammad. "I know what to do. I will call you when I need you." Standing alone by the sidewalk, he continued talking to himself, *I was only trying to pull their legs, bring them down a bit, and force them to be mellow with me. But if influenced by them, Anne Marie does not want to speak to me anymore. They will have to eat their pride. The shame will be so much. Anne Marie will need a shoulder to rest her head. Whose shoulder is better than mine to console her? Esaie is working at the bank. They already had their cars. Now they just bought a new van. One way or the other, something big is going on. I will get to the bottom of this. The jackpot is in that Igloo container. Whether it is money or drug, I'll find out.*

Takeema was not far from Mohammad. Listening to him and his friends, she suddenly understood that he was a dangerous man and whatever was going on with Esaie and his brothers was more serious than she thought. Mohammad was standing there gritting his teeth. Suddenly his facial expression became harder and harder; fire seemed flashing in his eyes. Behind that pole with her heart pounding, Takeema shivered with fear; this evil look was up to no good. She did not make a sound until he walked away. The moment his back disappeared at the end of the street, she started running back home as if she was running for her life. Convinced that Esaie had something that could compromise him, she wanted to warn him. In front of the building, she could not wait. She went right up and knocked at the door.

"My brother doesn't want to speak to you," said Hyppolite, who did not really know what was going on.

"This is a matter of life and death," said Takeema out of breath. "Please let me speak to Esaie."

"I am tired of you stalking me," said Esaie, coming out of his room. "I can't stand this any longer. You do not know how much trouble you have already caused me. Leave me alone. You are a human being for God's sake. Have dignity!"

"Believe me this time. This is not a joke. This is more dangerous than I thought. I want to warn you about Mohammad. He's planning—"

Without saying more, Esaie slammed the door and went to the living room, where Méralie was waiting for everybody for a quick talk.

Takeema went back downstairs, confused and stressed out. She lit one cigarette after another. You would think, instead of smoking, she was eating them. From the front of her building to the corner of the street, she walked back and forth over and over, waiting and hoping that Esaie would come out, even to go to his car. While waiting, she saw a man sneaking in the parking lot looking at the van. She could not stand still. She reentered the building with the idea to knock one more time, but she stopped halfway. In second thought, she did not want to get in trouble with Mohammad and his friends. Besides, going back upstairs and banging again at the door would not make any difference. As time passed, she bounced from fear and worries to frustration and fury until an idea came to her mind. She went back downstairs and stood across the street by the sidewalk.

Meanwhile, everybody was upstairs listening to Méralie who was not too indulgent in her speech.

"It has been twenty-four hours since this house is upside down. An atmosphere of tension is growing so thick around us that you can cut it with a knife. I do not understand my children anymore. My home has turned to a living hell."

"Mommy!" said Esaie, who did not know how to escape the conversation.

"No, no, no!" said Méralie annoyed. "Do not disturb me. I did not gather you here to question you. This is not an interrogation. When you judge that it is okay to speak to me, I will be ready to listen. I realize that you are not adolescents anymore. You are adults able to make your own decisions. You are responsible for your actions.

"Anne Marie mentioned that you are going through some difficulties. She did not specify. She just said that it is not a big deal, nothing to worry about, but your long and worried faces are saying otherwise. I only know one thing. There is no small problem. A problem is a problem. If you do not take care of it, it will grow on you like a pregnancy. You are three grown men, but I am still your mother. It is normal for me to be worried when something is wrong. I have this right, and I would like to give you a piece of advice.

"The only thing that doesn't have a remedy is death. I mean, if there is life, there is hope. It is a constant struggle. You must keep on trying and doing whatever can be done. As my old boss used to say, 'We are living in a world of wolves. It's a jungle out there.' Some actions require immediate and spontaneous reactions. This is human nature. I do not know what is wrong currently, but whatever the problem is, whether it is financial, health, or legal, do not underestimate it. You cannot sit back with this long and morose look on your face and wait for it to solve itself. Do not let your instinctive reaction exaggerate it either. It is necessary to maintain poise and calm rather than give in to panic and hysteria.

"Your father died when you were still young. I was alone trying to make a living and take care of you. I have tried to protect you, but it seems that I raised you the wrong way. You never brushed up with the real world to make you strong.

"I understand perfectly that you are not rocks. You are human beings with feelings. When problems hit, you feel threatened. It is normal that you react a certain way or even panic, but you need to come back to your senses. You need to use your brain and find a solution. Problems come and go. We need to face them with a positive mental attitude.

"Do not think you can always live freely day in day out, breathing, waiting for another day to come by. No! Problems hit sometimes, but don't you dare give up."

"But, Mommy, we are okay!" said Esaie.

"Don't you dare 'Mommy' me!" yelled Méralie a second time. "The most disconcerting is that I heard Mohammad was up here this morning to intimidate you, and you let him get away with it. I cannot believe I have four cowards as children. When I was a kid coming from school, if another kid hit me and I did not hit back, I got beaten again by my parents. I understand you were not raised in the streets. I am not asking you to use violence, but Mohammad is not smarter than you. I cannot believe that, because of his scheme, you throw your hands up in despair and you allowed him to step all over you. You are intelligent. You are smart. Act upon it consequently.

"If, deep inside, you know you did something wrong, please confess your sins to God first, and like my mother used to say, 'Fasten your belt and be a man.' Face the consequences. But if you are innocent and you come across things that are too hard, too unfair, things that can cause you to collapse, have faith. God is on your side. It may be uncomfortable. You may have to stretch, but you do not have to be bitter, spiteful, and negative. Do not lose the battle in your mind. Do what you suppose to do, and you will discover ability you do not know you have.

"If you do not step out of line, you do not violate the law. Take control of your life, and take control of your problems too. Remember you are children of God. He is faithful. He will not let you be tempted with more than you can bear. The storm will give way to the sun. That is all I want to tell you. Please think about it."

Méralie went back to her room, refusing to hear any kind of reasoning until her children decided to speak clearly to her.

Mohammad was still in the neighborhood. Just the idea that he would not see Anne Marie anymore drove him crazy. He went to the liquor store, got a bottle of Bacardi, and sat across the street. As she did not come out or answer her phone, he got furious and made up his mind. He just wanted to make sure the container was in there to alert the police. Everything looked simply. Only a matter of minutes. It started to get dark outside; executing his plan would be easy.

By 6:30 p.m. that Monday, he walked in the building for a definite conversation with them.

In his sick mind, he thought, *These men are passive, civilized, and too well educated to stand a scandal. Besides, Méralie had been going to the doctor. Her health might be delicate. If she found out what is going on, it would be even better. The family would have to step down from their pedestal of righteousness and submit to his demands or else. Depending on the circumstances, their secret would be brought to light, and everybody would know what was going on.*

All that time, Takeema was on alert. At six thirty-two, just minutes after Mohammad went upstairs, she also entered the building; but this time, instead of going up, she went straight to the basement.

When Mohammad knocked on the door, Hyppolite tried passively to get him to leave. The house was too tense for Méralie to have more worries. But with the maddening arrogance of someone who knew he was playing to win, he took advantage of the situation. He openly declared that he would not leave until he spoke to Anne Marie; that was his biggest mistake.

Wisdom is a virtue; it is not always good to underestimate people. Sometimes you do not know when you cross the line until you are on the other side. And of course, by then, it is too late. Mohammad had learned this lesson but the hard way.

He was standing at the door when Hyppolite grabbed him by his neck, dragged him down the steps, and pushed him out of the front the door. As he came back in, Hyppolite caught his chin with a fist and knocked him down. He tried to fight back but could not; he was getting hit like a punching bag.

The commotion got the attention of Tertulien and Esaie, who ran down the steps as fast as they could. Mohammad was knocked down, yelling and crying for help. Hyppolite was punching and kicking him with rage as if he wanted to discharge all the frustration accumulated in him over time. Instead of stopping the beating right away, the two brothers locked the entrance door and stood there watching Hyppolite let off steam, venting his anger. When they finally stopped it, Mohammad was twisting with pain.

"This morning, we made a complaint against you," said Esaie, bending over him on the floor. "The police are looking for you. This evening, you came back looking for trouble. Hyppolite should have killed you. Next time you come here, you will not go back out on your own feet."

Dragging on his leg with his clothes stained with blood, Mohammad managed to get out of the door and disappeared in the midst of the evening. Tertulien and Esaie went back upstairs, conversing with Hyppolite.

"Mohammad deserved the beating, but, man, you must control yourself. If we did not intervene, you would have killed him."

"When did you make that police report?" asked Tertulien.

"I didn't, but if Mohammad knew we had a complaint against him, he would think twice before going himself to the police and complaining about this beating."

Strange coincidence, Mohammad's beating was not the only beating that took place that evening.

Takeema went inside the building only for ten minutes. All suspicious, she came out by the basement door with a bag under her arm and crossed the parking lot in a rush while venting her frustration.

I was trying to help, but I do not care anymore. Esaie is a hypocrite and a liar. I always saw him as an honest and hardworking man. I would never think he was dealing with drug trafficking or stealing money from his job. Now, if he wants me to have dignity, he does not have to worry any longer. I will go away where he will never see me again. He will be sorry for humiliating me like that. This ungrateful man does not remember we were together and how much he was crazy for me.

But one thing is for sure, Mohammad is not smarter than I am. He is not laying a hand on any money or anything valuable that can be sold from that Igloo container.

As she stood by the sidewalk, waiting to cross the street, a man slapped her in the face and grabbed her by her arm.

"You are a bum, a dirty and miserable whore. You do not have any shame. I have been watching you. I know you are messing around with a man living in that building across the street. You were with him, right? This is the last time you disrespect me like that. I'm working hard all day long to give you whatever you want, but you have to prostitute yourself to satisfy your drug habits."

"I was not doing anything!" yelled Takeema desperately. "Help! Let go of me, or I am calling the police."

As Takeema was yelling, crying, and trying to run away, the man grabbed her hand, threw her inside of an old truck that was parked in front of the building, and took off.

Fear is the worst thing that can happen to a human being, thought Esaie. *It paralyzes your body and your mind. It turns you into an idiot. Any simple matter that would be resolved easily is blown out of proportion. Fear can drive you crazy.*

The three brothers finally realized that. Given a lot of thought to their mother's advice, they decided to act as fast as they could. It was already 7:30 p.m.; Tertulien had to get to Paterson to speak to Marie Louise, the mother of his son, Joseph. Without giving it one more thought, Esaie and Hyppolite decided to go along and take care of the package once and for all.

"Mother is right," said Esaie. "Some actions require an immediate reaction. That package has been a torment for us since yesterday. It should not still be here. We cannot let emotion overpower our reason, not anymore."

"The container is not in the van!" said Hyppolite. "Where is it?"

"I removed it from the van," responded Esaie. "It is still around, and it is still a risk. We need to act fast."

"We need to get out of here immediately," said Tertulien. "That thing will not stay here one minute more. Hyppolite is all dirty and wrinkled after the fight with Mohammad. While he goes upstairs to change, let us go get the package. There is a handbag somewhere there. We will just pack it in it."

"Let me drive," said Esaie. "We will get there faster."

"No, thank you," replied Tertulien. "You are too friendly and too popular. You have too many strings attached to your tail. We do not need any more surprises."

Esaie realized that Takeema had been a problem. He could not go out of the front door without her stalking him. So the plan was that he would go ahead, walking three blocks down to distract Takeema. Tertulien and Hyppolite would drive by, pick him up by Ocean Avenue, and continue their way.

Esaie and Tertulien ran down to the basement with a flashlight. They walked all the way to the back, entered the summer storage room, and headed to the container that was sitting right at the corner where they hid it. Rapidly they pulled the lid open and cautiously were ready to grab the package, but to their surprise, the container was completely empty. They were as shocked as the first moment they discovered the package, only this time they did not lose control.

Hyppolite was moving according to the plan. He got dressed, rushed out of the apartment, and was heading to the parking lot to meet Tertulien. He found him sitting on the front steps with his hands supporting his chin while Esaie was walking back and forth, pacing the sidewalk.

"What's up? Why are you not in the car? Why is Esaie still here?"

Tertulien and Esaie were looking at him with a livid and pale face, like they just got the biggest surprise of their life.

"What is it now?" yelled Hyppolite, nervous and curious.

"The package is gone, man!" said both, shaking. "Somebody broke in the basement and took it."

"What do you mean by the package is gone? How? Where is it?"

"When we discovered the thing yesterday afternoon," replied Esaie, "immediately I tried to get rid of it, but I couldn't. After that first attempt, I went back out last night, just for the same purpose. Unfortunately it seemed that Takeema, with Mohammad's help, was following me. At a moment of inattention, she got in the car and did not want to leave. At that point, I could not do anything. I drove back here and went to my room.

"I couldn't sleep. I was tormented. In the middle of the night, I went back outside and tried again to no avail. When I came back this morning, I removed the Igloo container from my car, but I did not put it back in the van. I had decided to hide it somewhere in the basement, in a room where they store the barbecue grills and summer things. The room is closed. It does not have any heat. Nobody goes in there until the end of spring. Even the super would not go there. He is taking care of the three buildings of the block. He does not live in this one.

"He usually comes here on Thursdays to inspect and take the garbage out. He would not come over unless there was an emergency. Today is only Monday. He did not stop by at all. Now I do not know who possibly saw me moving that container because, at that time, nobody was around."

"Damn it!" said Tertulien. "Whoever found that thing is going straight to the police. God! This is a curse."

"We need to calm down and think," said Hyppolite. "The only thing that would possibly link us to that package is the container. I am sure people have seen it. We need to get rid of it."

"But this container is kind of big to carry around. People will notice it."

"We don't have to go anywhere with that empty container. Today is Monday. It is recycling night. Let's fill it up with empty cans and bottles and put it on the sidewalk. Just do not take any of the cans and bottles we have used in the house. We do not want to have our prints and saliva on them in case of an investigation. Hurry up. We need to get to Paterson."

At fifty-one degrees, the weather was not bad. The forecast did not mention any snow or rain. The men immediately went down to the basement, grabbed the container, and put it out with recycling items in it. They then boarded the car to Paterson with Tertulien behind the wheel; it was exactly 7:00 p.m. Before they could even move out to the street, two police cars drove right in front of the driveway and blocked the gate. Soon the whole parking lot and the front of the building were filled with police officers with dogs, checking the cars and questioning people.

The three brothers got out of the car and stood there with the idea that, this time, they were in big trouble. Mohammad had fulfilled his threats; he reported the beating to the police and God knows what else he said against them. As the police ordered them to leave the parking lot, they went across the street and stood at the sidewalk to watch the activities. Their hearts jumped when the officers with flashlights and sniffing dogs approached the van. Since they did not find anything unusual, the squad moved into the building to continue the search. And the boys, instead of breathing easier, their worries were even greater. For the container was sitting right on the sidewalk. The thing was gone, but the dogs could have easily detected a smell or something if the police decided to check the recycling.

Meanwhile, life went on in the street. The intersections where the building was located were blocked to traffic, but people were passing by as usual. Some stopped at the other side of the street, craning their eyes and trying to find out what was going on.

Some did not even care. "It is just another drug bust. What is new?"

Among those people going by, there was a special person who happened to be in the area. He was a middle-aged man, skinny and tall. To judge him from the outside, he looked healthy. He never spoke to anybody or stood in front of any crowd in the streets to find out what was going on. Without paying much attention to anyone, his only business was with the empty cans he was collecting. He did not live in the area, but everybody in the neighborhood knew him for passing by every Monday evening at the same time. He never changed his itinerary: from the Greenville area, he usually took Bergen Avenue straight down and turned onto Communipaw, Harrison, Gifford, and so on. He would walk slowly but surely, pushing an old shopping cart with bags full of cans hanging on both sides.

That night, in front of the building, he displayed his usual indifference to all that police activity and the crowd of commentators standing by. With the cold weather and that long walk he had to put in, time was not to be wasted under any circumstance. He picked up all the cans from the Igloo container and left the glass bottles behind.

Walking away, he only made a few steps, stopped, and turned his head, thinking for one second. He walked back to the Igloo container, taking a time to check it out. He turned it around, looking at the bottom; he opened the lid and closed it back. A police officer who was watching the front gate suddenly blew a whistle and ordered him to move. Without contesting a word, he threw the bottles in another garbage can, picked up the famous Igloo container, threw it on top of his shopping cart, and continued while the police were still in the building with their sniffing dogs looking for anything suspicious.

-11-

Love Me, Love My Dog

Joseph was living with his mother, a brother and sister, and Maximilien, the stepfather. Marie Louise met him at work. She was working for a company as a general worker while he was the company truck driver. They soon fell in love and did not take long to move together. He lost his job six months after, and they relocated to Paterson.

When Tertulien got to Paterson, Maximilien was not home. Joseph had a mark on his face; he claimed that they sent him out for cigarettes and the store did not want to sell to him. He went back home, and they thought he was lying. The stepfather was drunk, and while arguing, he hit him in the face.

Esaie was annoyed. He did not want to blame Marie Louise over his brother; instead, he tried to advise them both.

"The stability of a home is important to the well-being of a child. It allows him to grow to his full potential in an environment of peace and trust with the parents' love and support. Unfortunately, this is not the case. You both have taken different paths. You are separated. Marie Louise is living with someone who does not get along with Joseph. Maximilien is an alcoholic. Joseph is not at peace. Being fourteen years old, this is a critical age. You cannot trap him inside like he is five. He goes to school alone. He has friends. Whether you like it or not, he has choices. He can easily accept peer pressure, listen to bad advice, and fall through the cracks like hundreds of other kids who live confused, betrayed, and angry. Or you can be more loving, more careful, supporting him, guiding him to be a decent human being."

"Parents get separated or divorced, and the kids suffer the consequences," continued Hyppolite. "It is very destructive for a child to be forced to live in a fatherless household where the father is replaced by a live-in boyfriend, a drunk, on top of that."

"You have a smart mouth," responded Marie Louise, upset by the comment. "Joseph is very hyper. He does not pay any mind to anyone. He does whatever he wants. Maximilien is a good man. He is not working, but he is doing his best to provide for the family. The main problem is Joseph's disobedience."

Tertulien took advantage of the situation to demand that Joseph come to live with him in Jersey City. Marie Louise was forced to sign custody over to him; otherwise, the boyfriend would go to jail. The problem was solved. Tertulien was happy to have his son now with him.

It had been a long and terrible day. On their way back home, the men did not want to talk because of Joseph's presence, but encountered thoughts were running in their minds faster than the car they were driving on that highway.

The fight with Mohammad created a kind of discomfort, for violence was not their strength. The disappearance of the package was a big question mark hanging in their minds; it was like a wound healed from the outside but that needed to be handled with care because the inside was still delicate. The presence of the police squad searching their parking lot and inside the building triggered a feeling hard to forget. And the most amazing, mysterious, and miraculous thing was the container that vanished right before their eyes seconds before an officer with a dog stopped on the sidewalk, just where it was sitting. The can collector was an angel; he was at the right place at the right time to pick it up and walk away. To them, destiny had met with luck right at their front steps to bring an unexpected but welcome relief in a crucial situation, in a moment of hell. What seemed to be unusual and weird was, during all that confusion, Takeema, the lady across the street, was not there. They did not notice her during the police activity or when they were going to Paterson.

Joseph coming home with his father brought a bit of animation to Anne Marie, who was sitting, lost in her room.

"Raising kids," she said, "requires love, patience, commitment, and dedication. Joseph was an obedient and docile kid before. It has been a while. He is on the defensive, running, hyper. Maybe the treatment he was receiving at his house changed him like that."

"When people fall in love," said Méralie, "they often express their desire to have kids one day. It is comforting to hear future parents talking about kids that would bring joy to their home. But nowadays the traditional family is coming apart. Child abuse is growing out of control. Therefore, delinquency becomes a real problem to society. When kids are growing in a hostile or abusive environment, they learn to be the same way. When they are neglected or mistreated at home, they react badly. They turn to friends, to the streets, looking for attention in all the wrong places. Parents need to take responsibility."

"Speaking about parent's responsibility," said Anne Marie, "the other day, I bumped into Ed, the new boy who lives down the street. He was coming from the park, bouncing his ball as usual, but he had a cigarette in his hand. When I questioned him, he answered that his brothers and sisters also smoke. Since they did not prohibit him, he thought it was cool to do it too."

"That is a shame," said Méralie. "This boy reminds me so much of Popo. He is going in the wrong direction. We should encourage him to visit us more often. We will be able to speak to him and counsel him."

"I do not advise that, Mommy. This boy has his own family. He is a minor. We do not want to get in trouble."

"*Beni soit l'Eternel*"—blessed be the Lord—"for my grandson!" said Méralie, changing the conversation. "I am glad he is now staying with us. We are not rich, but we have love. He will be better off here because it is difficult for a child to live under the same roof with a temporary father, a perfect stranger who views him as an inconvenience to put up with. This is the reason I never paid attention to any man after my husband's death. My children were not babies, but I did not want any stranger to live with them. *Aime moi, aime mon chien!*" Love me, love my dog!

"'Love me, love my dog.' What do you mean by that?"

"When you are in a relationship, you need to have consideration for things that are dear to the person you love. You cannot be in love with someone, and you are beating on his dog. Sooner or later, that will backfire. Either the dog will bite you, or his owner will hate you. If you should have consideration for a pet because you love his master, with more reason, you need to love his children who are his own flesh and blood."

"The parents do not know the damage they are causing when they are making decisions without thinking of the well-being of the children. I am working on a project for school. I would like to speak about the teenagers and the problems encountered in our society. It is especially important to me."

"I thought you completed your studies with Hudson County Community College. Wasn't this semester your last?"

"Yes. As a matter of fact, I might start working soon. This coming Monday, I have a job interview. But I still must present my exit paper to school."

"Good for you. You will get it," said Méralie. "But I noticed you have been crying a lot. Your eyes are all red. You are sad. Mohammad does not deserve so many tears."

"We are not talking about Mohammad, Mama," responded Anne Marie, running back to her room.

Méralie joined Joseph, who was eating in the kitchen, and started another conversation. Meanwhile, the men went back to the parking lot, doing another cleaning of the van. Although it was already cleaned and shiny from the day before, they wanted to make sure there was no trace of the package left. Tertulien kept on dusting and spraying and wiping and waxing with determination. He was working as if he wanted to wipe out the mere souvenir of that ordeal that started with the discovery of the package inside the van.

"The van is spotless," said Esaie, looking at it with satisfaction. "I wish I could do the same to my mind and clean it out completely of the memory of that unfortunate and worrisome incident."

"Today is Monday," said Hyppolite. "From yesterday afternoon to this moment, within twenty-four hours, we have known hell. It has been a roller coaster of emotions, panic, fear, worry, and even anger. The apparition of the package, as well as its disappearance, has been a surprise and a mystery. Now we do not have a clue of what is going to happen."

"Let's hope nothing happens," said Tertulien. "When Esaie placed the container in the basement, it was early in the morning. I have the feeling somebody was watching, and he removed it right away. Whoever took it, if he wanted to make a scandal, he would have enough time to do so. Don't you think?"

"But who took it? What for? Did he know what was in it?"

"These questions," replied Hyppolite, "I cannot answer. I do not think we will ever find an answer. It is better for us to turn the page and forget it. Like the Haitians said, 'Let us close the case and archive the folder.' We cannot dwell any more on this. We need to move on with our lives."

We need to move on with our lives! That last sentence particularly touched Esaie's heart, who always had a kind of bond with his brother. He looked at him with admiration and a kind of sympathetic feeling as if he were reading his mind.

"What about you, Popo? Will you be able to do the same? Would you put this and everything else behind you? Since January, you have been tormented by that terrible earthquake. I do not want to dwell on this or keep on reminding you the same thing, but I know it is still in your mind, and that affects your relationship with people. Would you put this behind and move on with your life?"

"I am trying. I don't know. It is not easy."

The week had passed, and everyone went back to their regular activity. It seemed life had timidly returned to Méralie's home. On Sunday after church, the boys were together inside the van, doing their weekly cleaning. Esaie stopped a minute to speak to Hyppolite

"Another thing particularly important I would like to ask you, Who is Hellen? How is she? What kind of person she is? What do you think about her? Do you have any feelings for her?"

Hyppolite stayed quiet for a while. He scratched his chin with a smile at the corner of his mouth. "Boy! So many questions! Hellen is nice. She is delicate and warm. As you look at her, she is just a regular girl. But I don't know why I cannot control the tremors of my heart before the sovereign sweetness of her smile. She becomes so attractive, so fascinating. She is everything you would want in a woman. She has an energy that naturally emanates from her person. I would say that she is like the morning sun on a beautiful day after the torment of a long and stormy weather. It is nice to be with her. But right now, I am trying to stay away. I do not want to get involved and afterward say goodbye. I don't want to hurt her feelings because I don't know how long I will be staying in the US. I have to go back to Haiti."

"After the description you just gave, how can you resist? I do not know if you are human or a rock."

"I don't know either," said Hyppolite, getting out of the van with his hands in his pockets. "I don't know."

"Leave him alone," counselled Tertulien. "He has made a lot of progress. Before, he was not talking at all. Last week, I was so surprised at his reaction with Mohammad. Little by little, we are getting our brother back. He is coming out of this morbid passivity that kept us all worried. Don't push him into a relationship he might not be ready for."

"Hyppolite needs to free himself from negative thoughts," replied Esaie. "Staying in the house all day long in front of a computer is not helping. Even working with the van, by 7:00 p.m., he usually comes back to the house with his mind stationed on hurtful experiences. I understand that he is more animated now. He even smiles sometimes, but sadness had become part of his everyday life. And that is not a life. He needs to learn to let go."

"What do you have in mind?"

"I don't know. Let me make a phone call to make sure," said Esaie, smiling. "Hyppolite needs a friend. I mean a charitable soul to hold his hand and help him through the end of this tunnel."

Anne Marie woke up the next day with a full calendar. The whole day was dedicated to Joseph. Hyppolite and Esaie didn't have children yet, and Joseph was her only nephew. She considered him like her little brother, or her son. At 8:00 a.m., she was ready to take care of business. She had to get a transfer from Joseph's school in Paterson and register him in Jersey City. She had not decided yet on which high school to choose. She also needed to buy him new clothes.

Everything needed to be done in a timely fashion because, the next day, she would start training with her new job. In this present time where finding a job was more difficult than finding a needle in a haystack, she did not want to miss the opportunity.

By 11:00 a.m., she was at Ferris High school with Joseph to register him. At the entrance, she met Benoit, an ex-school comrade, who was coincidentally there to take care of a matter for his little brother. He was a twenty-five-year-old man, tall, skinny, nice looking, and well-mannered. He was studying law at NJCU and was still playing basketball in his free time; he had been in love with Anne Marie since high school.

"Thank you so much for the flowers and the card you sent for my birthday. I can't believe you still remember my birthday. It was nice of you."

"How could I forget your birthday? I never lost track of you. I never gave up on you. I don't call you every day or visit you simply because I don't want to be inopportune."

"Thank you anyway for being so nice."

"I never stopped loving you, Annie. I do not think I ever will. I tried to forget you, but my heart will not allow me. Your image is engraved in my mind like a stone."

"Let's not speak about that," said Anne Marie. "You are a nice man. You deserve the best. Right now, I am not up for any conversations like this. Tell me, what you are doing here?"

"I am here for my brother, Henry. Since my mother's death, I have tried to pay more attention to be more supportive. You know, at this age, kids need someone to hang on to, to listen to, and to trust. As a big brother, I must be for him. He needs to know that I care."

"I always get a catch in my throat when I see adolescents running the street instead of being in a classroom. I sympathize with them. Very often, adults judge the youth according to their own criteria. They never tried to walk in their shoes. They even forget they were kids themselves. A lot of those young people get in trouble with

the law at an early age, and they lose the opportunity to have a normal life and become decent citizens."

"You are young still. I like your reasoning. You will make a good
mother."

"I feel lucky for having the mother I have," continued Anne
Marie. "My father passed away when we were young, my brothers
and I. Mommy is a strong and courageous woman. She has been dedicated to our well-being. I get angry when I listen to the news. Some
parents, for one reason or the other, really give up on their kids. It is
outrageous. For these reasons, I am trying to have more studies, do
more research about the youth. I chose the term youth advocacy for
my exit dissertation in school."

"Count on me for any help you might need," said Benoit.

They were sitting in the waiting room talking when Mohammad
showed up. He had a Band-Aid on his forehead and his lips.

"What happened to you?" said Anne Marie. "Did you have an
accident?"

"Why don't you ask your brothers? They will tell you better.
They are the criminals who almost killed me. Would you come with
me? I want to speak to you."

"I'm waiting on the secretary. I can be called at any time. I
cannot go out now. Besides, Joseph is with me. We cannot speak in
front of him."

"Your brothers hate me. I was about to discover their secret,
something illegal they are doing. But they did not want you and your
mother to know about it. For this reason, they beat me up. Look at
my face. These criminals almost killed me. Sooner or later, I will get
them for that. Make sure you tell them."

"I don't know what to think anymore. The other day, I witnessed
how you threatened them for no reason. You were overly aggressive.
They did not do anything to you. My brothers are not violent."

"Anne Marie, I want to speak to you because I want to know
what is going on between us. I have not seen you for several days, and
I swear to you they were the worst days of my life. I love you. I would
put my life on the line for you. Let us step outside for just a minute."

"When I met you," said Anne Marie with tears in her eyes, "I thought our love was forever. I was ready to give up anything to be with you. I saw in you the father of my children, the man I would love until the end of my life. I know my family didn't accept our relationship, but I never listened to them. I did not give up because I love you. I knew they would get used to it. I thought our love was strong enough to convince them. After all, this relationship was not with them. It was only between you and me. But you hate them so much you would rather see them in trouble. You were waiting for any occasion to hurt them. You do not understand, by hurting them, you are hurting me. I do not recognize you anymore. You have turned into a bitter and angry man. This is not the man I loved. It looks like you are empowered by a bad instinct. You will not hesitate to hurt. I think we should stop seeing each other for a while. We don't have to be enemies, but—"

"Don't you dare!" yelled Mohammad. "Don't you dare give me that let-us-stay-friends speech, not after all we have lived together. I know you love me as much as I love you."

"Mohammad, love me, love my dog!" said Anna Marie, moving two steps away.

"What are you talking about?"

"When you love someone, be ready to have consideration or tolerate even his dog. If you love me and you hate my family, there is no reason for us to be together."

Benoit was standing in the back. He could not hear them, but he was observing. As the conversation got more heated, he walked over to them and told Anne Marie the secretary was waiting for her. Joseph was already in the office. Mohammad thought Benoit was trying to get Anne Marie away from him. He threw a punch at him and missed. Benoit did not return the punch; he went back to his seat and decided to wait for Anne Marie and Joseph to walk them to the car just in case.

Yanique wasn't too happy either. Since the last events, she could not communicate with Esaie. This one, instead of coming home after work, went directly to Bayonne and invented a family problem without mentioning the ordeal he went through. He was relieved but did not feel completely liberated. The package could not walk out by itself. Deep inside, something warned him that it was not over. He was sure that the disappearance of the package was directly connected with Takeema's absence. They both disappeared the same evening, but where was she?

On two different occasions, he was about to go across the street asking for her, but he retracted. Not only did he feel guilty about looking for her; but if his family saw him going there or, worse, if the boyfriend knew, that would be a problem. Even if he were able to speak to her, what would he tell her about the package that would not raise suspicion?

I had better kept quiet, he thought. *I'll cross the bridge when I get to the river.*

Besides Anne Marie, who still felt hurt about Mohammad, things got back to normal. Hyppolite was still hesitant every time he had to take the van to work.

"Don't be so tense," said Esaie, addressing to him. "Try to relax. Everything will be okay."

"I am thinking of those two bums who left their package in the van, causing us so many headaches. You never know, while riding around, I might see them in the streets."

"Please don't even stop the van if you see them. Just keep on going. We need to put this unfortunate incident behind us completely. Try to think about things more enjoyable. Hellen, for example. Have you spoken to her lately?"

"No. I am debating if I should call her."

"I want to be honest," said Esaie. "Denying love without any good reason is just an excuse for emotional cowardice. And before you get mad and think that I am interfering in your private life, please check your messages."

Hyppolite went in the room and grabbed his cell phone; and after listening to Hellen's message, he stayed quiet, staring at the street through the window. Esaie got closer to him.

"Nobody can tell you that one is the girl for you, the woman you have to spend the rest of your life with. Maybe you are not looking for anyone. Maybe you hate commitment. But take it like this.

Suppose we are in the middle of the summer. You are working in your garden. Mandatory water restriction is imposed. The plants are withered. The forecast does not predict any rain. All you can do is clean the fallen leaves. If suddenly a wind picks up and raindrops start to fall, instead of complaining and being afraid of getting drenched, you should instead smile and hope for much more rain. Opportunity comes the same way. You are not looking for anybody. In fact, all you have in mind is sadness, bad memories, worries, anxiety, things that can make you sick, breaking your heart into pieces, like plants without water. But if suddenly someone special shows up, someone who makes your heart beat faster, opens her arms to you with a smile, do not punish yourself anymore. Consider that as a blessing, a rain of opportunity.

"After the ordeal you have gone through, after tasting the bitterness and unfairness of a miserable life, maybe your fate is changing. It is up to you to open your heart or not to that 'gentle morning sun' you were referring to. But if I were you, I would at least speak to Hellen. That message she left you is so touching."

"Hellen had her car fixed," replied Hyppolite. "She does not need help for the moment. I spoke to her. I might stop by later today."

"You don't have to drive the van. I'm going to Secaucus, and I can drop you there. Do not be rude. Bring flowers. Say you are sorry for not returning the calls. Tell her you do not have any excuses. Take your time. There is no rush. I will pick you up on my way back."

Hyppolite never forgot his brother's advice: "Simple but like a million bucks." He got dressed elegantly, bought the flowers, and left with Esaie, who dropped him at Hellen's in Secaucus. It was around 6:30 p.m.

Méralie was looking at the window when they left. The face of her children said it all. She turned her head up with a smile, giving thanks to the Lord who never failed her; he had brought peace back to her home. Lying on the couch, humming a song, she was thinking of waiting until they came back to at least bless them all and say good night.

The whole evening went by; Méralie went to her room and fell asleep. When Esaie finally came back home, it was 11:00 p.m.

"Where is Hyppolite?" asked Tertulien. "Weren't you supposed to pick him up on your way back?"

Esaie ignored the question and went straight to his room. As Tertulien insisted on asking questions, Esaie seemed to be annoyed.

"Listen! I love my brother. He has suffered enough. There is nothing I would not do to help him. Hellen is a nice woman, and she is in love with him. A little bit of happiness will not cause him any harm. Besides, Hyppolite is a grown man. He knows his way back. A taxi is at a phone call away. He doesn't need a babysitter."

Part 3
Garden State

Relax; breathe slowly.
See this pristine sky stretching above.
It is covered with pure azure.
This immaculate blue is its finest outfit.
Softly it is smiling.
Let's return the smile.

Welcome, Spring!

The silence of the winter is forgotten.
Mountains and hills don't remember
where they threw their heavy coats.
In full celebration, they join
the chorus of the tepid morning breeze
to sing along, reviving broken hearts,
giving praise for the glory of spring.
A slow-moving waltz meets the freshness
coming off the Hudson River.
New beginnings are in the air.
Everything is wonder and sweet promises.
The bright rays of the gleaming sunshine
caresses with ardor the first green touches
that the dawn hurries
Covered with the most beautiful flowers.
trees and bushes are dressed up
with red, pink, white, yellow, purple.
A spectacular mosaic of colors!
Tremendous explosion of beauty!
Nature awakens with a charm
worthy of admiration under the azure
and vivid sky of the Garden State,
a place where love blooms
like the flowers of the season.

-12-

Singing Worth Three Times Praying

They say true love only comes once in a lifetime and successful relationships are made in heaven. They say a lot about love. Everybody has their own story, their own experience, and their own memory about love. The truth is love can knock at your door at any time. It often surprises you and leaves you speechless.

No one knew much about Hyppolite's love life. Back in Haiti, he was a popular guy. But they never knew a steady girlfriend of his, nor did he ever mention he had a serious relationship with anyone.

When he came to Jersey City, he was just a mess, a nervous and tormented man. From then on, he had made a lot of progress. But the tragedy that had killed so many people, the earthquake that shook Haiti three months before, was still on his mind. He was still mourning and still feeling guilty for coming out uninjured while a lot of his close friends perished.

Hellen had expressed a pleasant feeling toward him. She had confessed to him her love. In return, he was not indifferent. He had felt a strong attraction to her. So far, he did not make any steps to get close. All Esaie tried to do was helping him to get out of this sad and boring daily routine that was turning him into a grumpy old man. He set up the stage for a face-to-face meeting with Hellen; the rest was up to him.

Hyppolite was still dragging his feet, feeling confused on what he should or should not do. Anything that would bring him joy or happiness, especially love, was not for him. And with that idea, he had tried staying away. So far, he had succeeded until that evening his brother drove him to Hellen's door.

When he rang the bell, Hellen was coming out of the shower. She had a pink bathrobe on and a towel wrapped around her hair. Hearing Hyppolite's voice, she ran to the door and opened it with a smile that made his heart jump. He had known her as beautiful, a serious office worker with suit, high heels, and makeup. But all wrapped in her robe, she was so pretty, so natural, and so attractive. He was looking at her, and his heart was racing. For a moment, he wanted to tell her that he loved her; he made one step forward and stopped right in his tracks. Since he could not say anything, he tried to put a face as normal as he could. As he stood there, shaking, his safest bet was the one he did not think about. He could have just turned around, grabbed a taxicab, and got the hell out of there. But the heart is so tricky; it seems to agree with your reasoning at times. And just when you are on the spot, when you need its support, it simply fails you.

At the door, Hellen grabbed his hand and took him to the living room, happy to see him. Hyppolite's initial plan was to give her a simple explanation for not returning her calls on time and book a date for a movie on Sunday, just to keep her happy. But something clicked in his mind; he did not pronounce a word of what he planned to say. He just stood there, mute, staring at her.

Hellen turned down the music she was listening to; she turned on a small crimson shaded lamp near the fireplace, throwing red glow around the room before going to the kitchen. She came back with two glasses and a bottle of wine. She sat by his side, smiling and waiting for him to say something. She took off the towel wrapping her head, drew her skinny fingers through her long wet black hair and poured the wine.

Hyppolite did not like to vent his feelings; but unable to look away from Hellen, he suddenly understood that he was not the indifferent, soulless, hard rock he had, for a long time, pretended to be. He wanted to tell her that it was not true that love did not interest him; he had been in love since the day they met. Completely captivated, he was following her with his eyes and unconsciously repeating her exact gesture. With his heart still racing, he moved closer. She smiled as he raised her hand to his mouth and kissed her fingers. As he stood in the living room in front of Hellen, her eyes locked in his, her body close to his; neither of them seemed to be able to move or say anything until he whispered her name. She finally pushed him gently and made a step back.

"Make yourself at home," she said. "Let me go upstairs to change. Enjoy the wine."

It was drizzling outside, and it started to get late. Hyppolite went to the window and glanced at the front yard. The darkness, already setting in, brought along a cool breeze, chasing the last strollers off the streets. A light rain mixed with the reflection of the light from the poles was tapping against the windows gently with its silver and rainbow drops. The winter was ending. It had been a genuinely nice day, but the stubborn evening weather managed to hold on to the cold with certain tenacity. Hyppolite pulled the curtains together and went back to the couch.

It was very cozy inside; Hellen had good taste. The long silky embroidered curtains, bordered with burgundy laces, so elegantly attached to the walls perfectly matched the flower arrangements sitting on the living room table. The wall decorations—some antique paintings revealing hill, mountain, ocean, landscapes, and scenes—reminded Hyppolite of the different dreams he had growing up. His eyes were drawn to the end table where there was a picture of Hellen with another girl who looked just like her. They were about ten years old, with the same hairstyle, wearing the same short-sleeve dresses with the same pastel- and pink-colored flowers.

This is probably her sister, he thought as he got up to take a closer look, *but she never mentioned they were twins.*

The music was still going on, filling the room with the melodious and unforgettable voice of Kenny Lattimore, Hellen's longtime idol. She came back and sat on the couch close to Hyppolite.

"You are so beautiful," said Hyppolite. "I love the music."

"Thank you," said Hellen. "Tell me about your music. What kind of rhythm do you have in Haiti? Do you dance?"

"In Haiti, we have all kinds of music," said Hyppolite. "We sing and dance like everybody. With the evolution of technology and Haitians bridging the gap with the rest of the world, we have access to all kind of cultures. Therefore, Haitians have music from all over the world, and they adopt a lot of them. After the folk music, the mainstream was the kompa and zouk, which are appreciated by the whole population. But for the Haitian people, singing and dancing go far beyond simple entertainments. Music can express in its beats the different aspects of human existence. It points out the joy, the hope we nourish, it also conveys the anguish, the mysterious torture of living and dying. It stands alone to communicate the symbols and phase of life.

"The Haitians use these means to praise God, to manifest their joy or happiness, to cry their pain and suffering, and to communicate with each other. My mother always said, 'Singing is worth three times praying.' This is part of our culture.

"For instance, you can complain about a problem for a long time. You shout it to everybody. Chances are they don't pay too much attention. The fact is people have their own misery. They had already heard so much they have heard it all. This is not carelessness or selfishness. They are only tired of bad news. But once you borrow the notes of a song to express the way you feel, they will stop to listen. The lyrics will touch some hearts. The message will make its way through. To me, communicating your feelings through a song or with the help of a musical instrument, like the tambour, tam-tam," he said as he made a hand drumming gesture, "is like butter that makes the bread easier to eat."

"Do you sing?" asked Hellen.

"Unfortunately, I don't. Maybe that is the reason I suffer a bit more than others. I do not express my feelings very often. But I would like to ask you a question."

"Go ahead," said Hellen, waiting

Hyppolite got up, offered his hand to Hellen, and said, "Would you like to dance with me?"

Hellen hesitated. She looked at him for a while and finally got up to meet his eyes. His hand felt electric against hers; she blushed.

He kissed her on the cheek, and timidly they started to make some steps. Soon they found themselves softly moving in the rhythm to the music:

> For you, there are no words or ways to show
> my love
> Or all the thoughts I am thinking of

With his arm around her shoulder, he gently pulled her toward him. Though she felt embarrassed at first, she did not resist. Instead, she closed her eyes, leaning into him, dropping her head onto his shoulder.

In the warmth of that room that surrounded them with flowers and curtains, they did not know how long they danced. Lost in each other's arms, there was not any room for neither reasoning, worry, nor sadness. The flowers that Hyppolite brought fell on the floor without their notice. The phone was ringing off the hook; only they and their love mattered. The magnetism that inexorably attracted them to one another, the sweat in their palms wanting to touch one another, the euphoria of being together, and the fire running through their senses, burning their heart, all came together in an explosion of passion, a rainbow of emotions—the miracle of love. Hyppolite found himself holding Hellen in his arms, and to both, life was worth living.

Anne Marie woke up early in the morning; that Wednesday was her first day of work. She was elegantly dressed in a gray suit with black shoes and purse. She went to the room looking for her brothers; she needed the blessing of everybody in the family to build her confidence. She was happy to get the job, ready to start, but she was as nervous as a kid on his first day of school.

"Don't worry," said Méralie. "You will be okay. I was around your age when I started working at the courthouse. I remembered my first day of work as if it were yesterday: I was worried about my English. I had difficulty communicating with people. But thank God everybody was patient with me. It did not take me long to learn the job and improve my English. The rest of the story, you know it. I raised my kids working there, and I retired after twenty-five years of service. Go with confidence. May God bless you."

Esaie and Tertulien did not wake up happy like Anne Marie. Instead, they were a bit worried; Hyppolite did not come back home. They had called him several times; his cell phone was off. When Anne Marie came into the room asking for him, they invented a story. She did not pay much attention because she was too excited about her first day of work. But would they be able to also lie to Méralie?

Tertulien was about to leave for work. Esaie approached him at the door.

"What do you think happened? Hyppolite didn't come back home, and he is supposed to take the van out today."

"How would I know?" replied Tertulien. "Hyppolite is not sneaky like you. You used to stay out all night and come back quietly at 3:00 a.m. like nothing happened, and Mother never noticed."

"That was a long time ago. Since I met Yanique, I am not the same anymore, but we are talking about our brother here, not me."

"It is your call, big man," replied Tertulien. "Find an explanation for Mother. She will notice Hyppolite didn't sleep here."

"Why are you so worried?" said Esaie. "Mommy had to understand that we are not kids anymore. This is the biggest problem of the Haitian women! They want to keep their children forever under their wings. We are all grown men. We shouldn't even be here, living together as if we were six years old."

"I'm late for work," said Tertulien, closing the door behind him. "I don't want to argue this morning. You broke it. You fix it. Just do not let Mommy get upset. I don't want her to get sick."

Esaie was scratching his head and wondering what to do before Méralie started asking too many questions. Hyppolite did not answer his phone. He tried to call Hellen; she did not answer either. Meanwhile, he was looking at his mother sitting in the kitchen with a cup of coffee, and he was looking at the van standing in the parking lot. Feeling guilty for pushing and taking Hyppolite to Secaucus, he grabbed his key and left before Méralie noticed Hyppolite's absence. Driving to work, he could not stop complaining.

I don't understand Hyppolite. He never acts like a normal human being. When he is sad, he is sitting in a corner of the house like a poor, defenseless soul ready to die. He would not look outside, not even through the windows. Yesterday, for the first time, he went to visit a woman, and now he completely forgets his way back home. What explanation would I give my mother if, by this afternoon, this bum does not come home?

-13-

Do Not Be Too Hard-Hearted

Since Mohammad got into the fight with Hyppolite, it seemed that he had learned his lesson. He did not go back to the house, but he did not give up. Now he was determined more than ever to make peace and escape with Anne Marie out of Jersey City. He went by her school and by the restaurant she was working looking for her; no one had any information about her. He kept on calling and sending messages without response. His last resort was Takeema; she was always in front of the building watching when Esaie was coming in and out. She should be able to tell him something about Anne Marie, so he went across the street and rang Takeema's bell.

"What do you want?" yelled someone from inside.

"I would like to speak with Takeema please."

A man mashing a piece of cigar between his lips opened the door to let him in. As Mohammad entered the apartment, a strong odor of alcohol and tobacco hit him right away. He looked around. The place was a complete mess you would think of an area of disaster. From the two wooden chairs that were in the apartment, one was knocked down, and the other one with broken legs leaned against the wall. Dirty clothes and sneakers were thrown all over the floor and the couch. On a small table by the corner of the room were more than a dozen crushed, empty beer cans of Coors and Miller Lite along with a crystal-clear ashtray overflowing with cigarette butts. Empty containers of pizza and Chinese food were scattered all around the living room and the kitchen. There was not any space to even sit.

Some of Takeema's clothing was hung by a nail on the inside door. Parts of the walls had holes punched in them.

The man was drunk; he went into the bedroom, grabbed a baseball bat, and walked toward Mohammad like he wanted to kill him.

"I am glad you are here today!" he yelled, threatening him. "I did not know where to find you. You are the one who has been seeing my woman, aren't you? I know Takeema had someone with her last week when she was coming out of that building across the street early that evening. You are the one she had been messing with. You are the cause of this disgrace. Everything that happened is your fault."

Mohammad stared at him with a perplexed expression. "What disgrace? What happened to Takeema? What are you talking about? I do not live across the street. I come to this neighborhood to visit my girlfriend. As a matter of fact, I want to speak with Takeema because I want some information about Anne Marie, my girlfriend."

Suddenly the man staggering under the influence of alcohol threw a bottle in the direction of Mohammad, who narrowly dodged the shot.

"Takeema is not here. She moved back to Mississippi with her relatives. I do not want to see you wandering in the neighborhood looking for my woman. Do not ever come back here ringing my bell anymore, or I will kill you."

Mohammad ran out of the apartment, thinking, *This man did something to Takeema. She would have not moved and left her belongings behind. This is crazy. He probably killed her. He doesn't want anybody to even mention her name. He just doesn't want to raise suspicion.*

It was around 4.30 p.m.; Mohammad was nervous and confused. Sitting in the Dunkin' Donuts at Journal Square, he couldn't get his mind off the grimacing face of the man who stated that Takeema moved out of Jersey City. He was sure the man was lying. Deep in his thinking, he was drinking a coffee while staring blankly at the streets through the windows.

From afar, he saw a woman walking down Sip Avenue. Elegantly dressed, she looked like one of these executive bank managers working in the area. At the intersection of Sip and Bergen Avenue, she crossed the street and continued Bergen Avenue. It was only then

Mohammad came back to his senses and realized that woman was Anne Marie, whom he had been so actively looking for. He suddenly jumped up his seat, heading to the door. While running out of the restaurant, he knocked down some chairs and did not even look back. He flew across the street and kept on running until he reached her.

"Annie! Annie, my love. Let me speak to you for a minute. I have so much to tell you. Let us sit in one of these restaurants. We will be able to have a better conversation. If you do not want to eat, my car is parked up the street. We can sit there and talk. Please, do not say no. Let us not stay in the street."

Mohammad was on his knees begging. Some kids passing by stopped to watch what was going on. Anne Marie was looking at the kids laughing. She would have liked to disappear and get away from Mohammad to stop the scene; but she knew, wherever she went, he would not stop following her. Like someone caught in the rain, she was standing there surprised and embarrassed.

"Forgive the poor boy," said a man passing by. "Don't be too hard-hearted. Don't you see he is on his knees?"

"You are making a spectacle in the streets," said Anne Marie, pulling Mohammad by his arm. "Why are you so overexcited? It looks like you just escaped death. Are you running away from the devil?"

"I came across the devil just twenty minutes ago."

"You are acting so weird. What is wrong with you?"

"Annie, I cannot go to your house anymore. I have been looking for you at school and at your job. No one would give me information. I sent you letters. I called. I left messages, and you have not returned my calls. I'm desperate. I don't know what to do."

"Mohammad, we already talked about this. Our relationship is not working. We cannot continue like this."

"Annie, I know that I have caused you pain. I am sorry. You did not deserve that. I will be sorry for the rest of my life. I hate myself for that. We were so much in love. We were so happy. I hope there is still room for forgiveness in your heart. Please, in the name of that love, forgive me."

"Mohammad, I am in a rush. Please go on your way. I have a lot to do. I need to get home."

"If you send me to hell, I will go, but I will still love you," said Mohammad. "I myself have been thinking about leaving New Jersey, but how would I go without you? Where would I find a woman like you? I love you."

"Mohammad!" said Anne Marie with sadness.

"You know how much I love you. I am a tormented man. My life is upside down. I cannot live without you. I cannot take a breath without thinking of you. Please, Annie. Let us go away, out of Jersey City, a place where we can live quietly, away from family and friends. We are not little babies anymore. We can settle somewhere together. I will do whatever you want me to. We were so happy. It was a dream come true. Life is short. It is tough. Do not discount what we have together. We can have the greatest love affair ever, or we can live apart in misery with our hearts broken. It's up to you. Our destiny is in your hand."

Anne Marie finally accepted to speak with Mohammad for five minutes, just to make sure there was not any misunderstanding. She was clear in her position; their relationship had no future. But Mohammad, for knowing her so much, was using the right words to touch her heart. He was pleading for the sake of their love, looking her straight in the eyes.

Sitting in the car, struggling with her feelings, Anne Marie was confused and sad. Encountered emotions overflowed her heart. She did not want to choose between her heart and her family. She was looking at him with tears in her eyes. Mohammad, as a persuasive man and a determined seducer, sensed weakness in her. He felt a kind of hesitation and confusion behind her demeanor. He understood she still loved him. He tried to push a bit forward, putting more pressure just to grab a positive answer from her. As he was hugging and kissing her, she did not stop him. Without saying a word, she got out of the car and kept on walking.

Before he could stop himself, Mohammad made a few steps after her, shouting, "I love you, Annie!"

He stood there for a while, watching her leaving.

The seed is sown, he thought. *Let her sleep on it. Give her time.*

He went back to his car and started the engine when a friend approached him.

"What is up?" he asked.

"What is wrong with you?" said the man, annoyed. "Don't you remember we had a meeting? Everyone was there except you. You didn't even answer your phone."

"Damn it!" exclaimed Mohammad, hitting his forehead. "I completely forgot."

"John is angry. You are working on everybody's nerves. This is not the way we operate, and you know it. I do not recognize you anymore. Who is this woman that robs your memory?"

"This is not in your business!" yelled Mohammad, who forgot himself for a while. "Sorry, do not worry. There is no problem."

-14-

A Date with Spring

Méralie, whose advising had become a habit, had always a word of wisdom for the young adults of her church.

"Love has a strange way of imposing itself and making its point. It intervenes in a person's life, keeps two people together as if they were destined to be with one another. It is inexplicable. You would think it is irrational, absurd, and that is the beauty of it. Life is everything and nothing at the same time. God put love to spice it up and make it worth living. Thank God for love. It is strange. It is marvelous. We do not know where love comes from, but if you believe that it has reached your path, do not let it pass you by. Don't let the opportunity to love and to be loved pass by."

These words came as a revelation in Hyppolite's and Hellen's lives. Coming from different backgrounds, they met accidentally and fell into each other's arms; and to them, it seemed that life had stopped around them—the world had stopped moving. The beauty of spring had knocked at their door, reinforcing their love and bringing a new accent of serenity in their life. Forgetting the rest of the world, they had eyes only for each other. They genuinely believed they had found paradise; they were happy.

When Hyppolite went back home, it was only to visit his mother. He would always have an excuse: he was terribly busy, he had a lot of running around to do, etc. The truth was he was moving away. Like how the cat carries her kittens one by one, he was emptying his closet little by little. As the winter was coming to an end, the heavy jackets made their way from the dry cleaners to Hellen's closet.

All through March, spring was crawling like a baby. Suddenly it showed up with a strong and active presence in the air, contributing to the joy and the magic of the moment, bringing its approval and more enchantment to the happy couple.

The nature came out of the lethargy of winter. The green color was right on schedule, rejuvenating the grass, the bushes, and the backyard's and front yard's gardens. The vines and their flowers were crawling back up, covering the fences that were stripped naked by the rigorous cold.

Hudson County has its own date with spring; it is a love affair. There is no need for a calendar or the groundhog to check its arrival. You can feel it and smell it right from the air. From Bayonne to North Bergen and Kearny, the still-shy sun flirts with the front yards, which don't hesitate to exhibit the young leaves of their full-of-sap bushes covered with the most gorgeous buds. People passing by come and go with a glimmer of happiness that is obvious. It is the truth; the seasons have the great ability to reflect on the mindset. When it comes to spring, it always brings animation and good humor.

As it gets warmer and warmer, the young folks regain the streets with their shorts, their décolleté, their happiness, and their energy, contributing to the joy of the season. The outdoor life starts with the most popular songs, the new arrivals from the department stores, and the most exciting movies from the theaters. Most of all, spring is the time for love, friendship, and adventure. Somehow the spirit and the mind are set free, and people are ready to welcome the benefits and the enjoyment of the green nature with an open heart.

Three weeks had gone by. Hellen and Hyppolite were practically living together. For the sake of this relationship and in the name of love, they had closed their ears to gossips, to reproaches, and even to advice. On Monday morning, they were getting ready for work. They had to drive to Jersey City to their respective activity. Going out to the car, they stopped to look at the rosebushes in the front yard. The plants had started to open their first flowers.

"These roses never missed a date," said Hyppolite, smiling. "They are messengers of love going by. They are here just for a moment, a moment passing in time. They stopped at your front yard right on schedule to bring us a message from spring and acknowledge our union. Before they leave, let us capture their freshness and imprint it on our love forever."

Hyppolite ran back inside and grabbed a camera. They stood up by the plants with the flowers surrounding them and, cheek to cheek, took a nice shot.

"When we first met," said Hellen, "I knew right away you were something special. You had that charm, a kind of sweet mystery I could not discern. Now I see what a truly romantic and amazing man you are, always uplifting and loving in everything you do. You are beautiful from inside all the way through."

"I love you so much," said Hyppolite, kissing her. "I can't picture life without you. We need to take in account all the promises of the season. Let your hand rest in my hand, and let us contemplate the future while enjoying it. To me, spring is the most beautiful, the most romantic of the year. And from what I have already seen, I think enjoying it in New Jersey is a breathtaking experience."

Hyppolite took Hellen to work and went to pick up the van at his mother's. He met Esaie at the parking lot and stopped for a while, speaking to him.

"I think it is time we have a talk," said Esaie with a serious tone. "I would like to know what you think you are up to with that Hellen. It has been two weeks since you went there. I thought you were going to visit. Maybe in the long run, establish a good friendship with her until you both decide that you are comfortable with each other and ready for a steady relationship. But no, as soon as you get there, you forget about your way back home. Now you come here by accident. It seems that you are trapped there."

"'That Hellen'? Now that is the way you call her. If I remember, you are the one who pushed me to go to her house. Do not take this as a reproach. I am infinitely grateful."

"Please do not get me in trouble with your mother," replied Esaie. "We were talking about a friend, someone to talk, to rely on.

I did not ask you to move out of the house. Now what is going to happen with the van?"

"Do not worry about the payment of the van," replied Hyppolite, walking away. "Now I have decided to work harder than I ever did."

"I forgot how serious and honest you always have been," said Esaie. "If she really loves you, I am happy for you."

"Do you believe in fate? Hellen has changed me in profound ways. I think fate has brought us together. I feel like an adolescent around her. I am surprised by myself. I am not the person I thought I was. I am not talking about anything material. I do not even know how to describe it. I regained confidence and peace. You may never know how much darkness she has helped me dispel."

"In just two weeks, Hellen has done all of this! Oh, boy, you are madly in love. Be careful. I just do not want you to get hurt."

"I will talk to you later," said Hyppolite, ignoring his brother's last statement. "I must see Mommy."

It was already 8:00 a.m. Anne Marie was about to leave for work. She opened the door just the moment when Hyppolite was stepping in. She embraced him in a rush and ran away.

"Why is she acting like that?" asked Hyppolite. "She did not even say a word to me. It is like she is avoiding me. This is not her. What happened?"

"Anne Marie has been weird for days," said Méralie. "I do not understand her anymore. She is jumpy, tense, unfocused. When she is in her room, she locks herself inside as if she is hiding something. While speaking to her, you must repeat yourself five times before she answers one question. It seems that she is not listening. She is on another planet. Something is going on. I do not know what it is exactly."

"I am worried about my sister. I think the whole family should get together and have a face-to-face conversation with her."

Méralie put down the rag she was cleaning the kitchen sink and turned around. She looked Hyppolite straight in the eyes, her facial expression becoming, for the first time, somewhat less than kind.

"Anne Marie is not the only one keeping me worried in this family. I would like to know what is wrong with you. What is going on? You are living with us. We all know you are going through some difficult moments. We are with you, and we love you. But it seems you do not care about anybody. Some days, I do not even see you at all. When you come here, it is just for a moment. Some nights, you do not even sleep here. The other day, I was in the mood for spring cleaning. I had the surprise of my life when I found your closet empty. One by one, you took your clothes away like a thief.

"When I tried to speak to Esaie, he started scratching his head, backing up, changing the conversation. Only Tertulien mentioned that you have a girlfriend. I am your mother, not your enemy. If you are planning on moving, I should be aware of it. I know you are a grown man. You can do whatever pleases you. People do crazy things sometimes in the name of love. I do not know who that girl is. But a woman who encouraged you to move with her secretly, leaving your home without your family being aware, is not a good woman."

"Mommy," said Hyppolite, "I did not plan to have a girlfriend or move out of the house. Everything happened so fast that I am still trying to comprehend and adapt myself to the situation. I met Hellen by accident through one of my customers. Her car broke down, and she needed somebody to drive her home.

"I was a real mess at that time. Long after the earthquake, I was so overridden by emotion. I was so affected that I was feeling the movement of the ground under my feet, still. From time to time, my friends' faces asking for help while I was standing there not able to do anything were flashing back to me. I could not describe my state of mind. I was plagued by guilt, deep-rooted fear of life. I felt guilty for being alive. I was so deep in my misery that I was reproaching God for keeping me alive. The only thing that restrained me from doing something crazy was your love, your faith, and your amazing strength.

"Then I met Hellen. I did not pay too much attention. I was not in the mood for romance. Besides, we had two separate lives—I mean, two different backgrounds. This woman is well settled. I did not even know why she was interested in me. I have benefited a lot from her advice. But her love, her patience, and her understanding have set something free inside of my heart. She has made me understand that I should be thankful I am alive, that maybe my mission is not over. If I need to help my family and friends, I must keep my head on my shoulder. I do not have any right to give up. If I am still breathing, life is still available to me. All depends on the effort I make to extend my hands toward life.

"I finally realized how harmful and negative my emotions and my behavior were. They were not only bad for me but also harmful to my family, my surroundings, and the people who care for me. This woman has been an anchor in my stormy seas, a star that illumined my darkest night. Her company has deepened peace and strength in my soul."

"Popo!" said Méralie with a more slow and softened voice. "How much do you know her? If this woman really likes you—God bless her—I am sure I will love her too. But you know my opinion about this. I like to make things right."

"Hellen is a good woman, Mommy. I know her well enough, and I love her. I do not know what would have happened to my life if I had to miss her one day."

Méralie was listening to her son; she was frightened. She knew Hyppolite was traumatized by that terrible earthquake, but she also knew he was not the kind of man who got involved every now and then with a woman. He was a serious and somehow delicate man, but she had no idea that he was capable of such depth of feeling. Never had he expressed himself that way about a woman. She shook her head side to side.

"Oh, my sweet Jesus!" she exclaimed. "Hyppolite is in love."

Anne Marie was sad for all the events that happened before in the family. Since the weather started to warm up, instead of going home after work, she had taken up the habit of going window-shopping in the Journal Square area. She would walk down Summit Avenue all the way to St. Paul Street and walk back home by Bergen or Kennedy Boulevard. But instead of feeling better, somehow she felt lonelier. Any flower stand, any ice-cream parlor, any movie theater, and even window shopping reminded her the good old days when she was swept out off her feet by the man she loved.

But since Mohammad had proposed to escape out of Jersey City with her, she had been tormented. Like a virus injected into her veins, the idea was working in her, affecting her behavior and her relationship with her family. She was already twenty-one years old. She was free to do whatever she wanted with her life. She could have packed up and left. But the way she was raised, the family ties weighed much more than she thought.

First Joseph was now living with them; Anne Marie had been doing a lot of reading on raising children. She had been passing information to Tertulien about discipline, which did not include beating a child for a mistake. It was rather a process by which the child learned what was acceptable and appropriate within his social reality.

But since she had the terrible news that two teenage boys from the neighborhood had been beaten and almost were killed in a drug-related incident, she was worried about her nephew. She took the responsibility of watching over him very closely, making sure his homework was done, his bedtime respected, and his meetings with the church youth program regular. Her effort had started to bear fruits because Joseph was calmer and more focused than before, and she was proud. She did not want to miss that.

Besides, Méralie's presence and her constant words of wisdom were like a soul's guiding light in the family. All those instructions had kept Anne Marie from stepping away and making a quick decision. The more she was thinking, the more she was ambivalent and nervous. She would like to divide herself in two to be in the house with the family and to fly far away with Mohammad to live their life happily ever after. For the moment, she was not sure of anything. At home, she locked herself in her room, making the inventory of her clothing for when she decided to leave. At the same time, she did not return Mohammad's calls; she needed more time to think. Besides, it had been a while since Mohammad stopped coming over. She did not want the family to have any suspicions that she was still in touch with him.

Méralie was in the habit of getting the family together for meetings when something troubled her. The following Sunday after church, she took advantage that. Esaie, Tertulien, and Anne Marie were home to debate the sudden relationship of Hyppolite and Hellen that had become an issue for her.

The family spent a while turning around the subject. Méralie would rather see her son fall in love with a girl from the church.

"A woman who fears the Lord, she shall be praised," she said. "A good wife has more value than gold and rubies. The heart of her husband safely trusts her. She does him good and not evil all days of her life. Her children rise and call her blessed. Her husband also praises her." This is the word of God.

According to Tertulien, "Hyppolite is a sensitive man, somewhat delicate. He has been through so much. Since he was raised in Haiti, he would be better off with a Haitian woman. With the same cultural background or way of life, they would be more compatible to each other."

Esaie did not want to say anything about Hellen. "Hyppolite is acting like a fool," he said. "Rushing too fast into something is not a good idea. In a relationship between a man and a woman, the best advisor is time."

After a good hour of debating, giving their opinion, the family concluded that Hyppolite was a grown man. What was already done was done; they did not want to force him to come back to his decision. He was taking a chance with a woman. The family decided to support him and pray that he was happy. If Hellen wanted to get close to them, they would do their best to welcome her and make her feel like she was a part of the family. All would be for the sake of Hyppolite, who had suffered enough. If anybody deserved to be happy, it should be him.

Anne Marie, all that time, did not pronounce a word. Carefully she was measuring every word and passively taking notes of everybody's statement. When they finally asked her opinion, she went off the hook to show her discontent.

"Hyppolite just met a woman that nobody knows. Quietly he removed his belongings from the house and moved in with her. Now everybody in this family justified his bad deed in the name of love. You feel that he deserves support. You are all ready to accept this woman with open arms. It is like the whole family wants to praise him and give him a trophy for his action.

"I do not have anything against Hyppolite. He is my brother, and I love him. If he is happy, I am happy for him, but what about me? Why does everybody hate Mohammad so much? Just because he loves me, he deserves to die. He cannot even visit me in this house because all three of my brothers mistreat him and are threatening to beat him up. Why so much discrimination? Is it because I am a woman? Do you want to keep me forever hostage in this house? I thought you people cared for me, but since you don't, I don't have to accept this any longer."

Before anybody had time to reason with her, she grabbed her pocketbook and ran out of the door.

-15-

A Place to Fall in Love

There is no doubt that, wherever love is growing, the goodness of nature is always an accomplice, supporting and backing up happy people. And when it comes to nature's goodness and beauty, the state of New Jersey is one of the best in the country.

After a rough winter where people practically lived indoors going from home to work, the outside life came as a blessing. Hellen liked traveling, visiting different places and mixing herself with the world. So time had come to go out and enjoy the warmth and the natural delight of outdoor places. She was thinking about staying in the state that summer. Hyppolite came from overseas not too long ago; he practically did not know the state. So instead of going elsewhere, it was decided they would use their vacation time to explore Garden State. As they were planning their itinerary, Hellen was trying to give a glimpse of some attractive parts of the state.

"New Jersey can be thought of as five separated regions," she said, "some more natural and picturesque, some more original and exotic than the others.

"Pine Barrens is a hidden treasure. Stretched across southern Jersey, it supports a unique spectrum of life, including orchids and carnivorous plants. With its heavily Florissant area of coastal plain, the sandy soil that makes it unique in the region protects a natural aquifer, supporting the purest water in the state. Unlike any other natural habitat on earth, it is blessed with ecological resources able to attract visitors from all over the world.

"The Delaware Bay lies just beyond the Pine Barrens beauty. It is perfect for a summer weekend. Backed by bountiful farms with their pick-your-own fruits and vegetables, you will not want to miss it."

"What about the Skyland?" asked Hyppolite.

"What can I say? It is interesting as well. Uplifted land, rolling hills, and mountains characteristic of North Jersey, it has a diverse geography filled with lakes and rivers. It is one of the biggest tourist attractions."

Armed with a map, Hellen and Hyppolite navigated the whole state, conversing one by one about the different regions—their ecology, art, culture, landmarks, and specialties. For having been to those places, Hellen took a real pleasure speaking about them. She was bursting with pride.

Instead of going through general information, she put herself up as a real teacher, an eyewitness giving good testimony of the attraction centers. Most of all, she particularly insisted on the cordon bleu restaurant where they could delight in products freshly harvested from the farms. Hyppolite, from time to time, would intervene to complete some information with specific details that surprised her.

"My goodness," she said, "it seems that you know more than I do. Have you been there before?"

He had not physically been to those places, but his constant thirst for knowledge had opened the door to the world. When it came to natural geography, population, and culture, he was especially interested. How could he pass up on New Jersey, the state he had been living in since he came back from Haiti?

The following day, while he was working, Hyppolite dropped off some people on Fairmont Avenue. It was around 10:00 a.m. The kids were in school, and the working population would not be out until the afternoon. Except for some police cars going by with their sirens, everything was quiet. Since he was in the neighborhood, he continued his way to visit Méralie, who was still complaining about his absences.

Soon he spotted Edmond, the boy who just moved in up the block, standing at the corner of Monticello and Jewett Avenue. This particularly caught Hyppolite's attention because he was a good friend of Joseph, his nephew, and, at this time of the day, he should not be standing in the street. He blew the horn, calling him. He did not answer; his head was turned the other way. Feeling that something was wrong, he parked the van for a minute just to make sure that Edmond was okay. As he was walking toward him, he saw him crossing the street to meet Mohammad, who was coming from the opposite direction.

Hyppolite instinctively stopped and went back to the van. He was looking at them through the retro visor but could not hear their conversation. Mohammad spoke with Edmond for a while, like he was giving him instruction. He then pulled money out of his pocket and handed it to him before letting him to go. Hyppolite become puzzled. Something was really going on. Mohammad resurfaced in the neighborhood, using this boy who was in and out of his mother's house; he was up to no good.

It was midspring when Hellen and Hyppolite started to go out, visiting the countryside while enjoying each other's company. Every weekend, they would travel by car; and without rushing, they would make frequent stops for coffee. Hellen, who never left home without her camera, would take a real pleasure taking the most beautiful shots while admiring the blooming nature.

During this time of the year, New Jersey is particularly interesting. Trees and bushes seem to be celebrating in a slow-moving waltz with the gentle breeze coming from Hudson River. Covered with the most beautiful flowers, they are dressed up with red, pink, white, yellow, and purple, forming a spectacular mosaic of colors, contributing to an explosion of beauty under the azure and vivid sky of the Garden State.

Friday afternoon is the time where the traffic is usually heavier than any other day of the week. Cars, vans, and trucks are flying by from all over heading to different places in the countryside. People take the roads by storm. Families, couples, and single adults are looking forward to getting a well-deserved fun weekend or a quiet retreat.

It was around four in the afternoon when they left that Friday, heading to countryside. From the turnpike, they were running simply fine; the traffic was excellent until I-95 south, where it started to slow down. Bumper to bumper, they were going less than twenty-five miles an hour on the highway where the speed limit was sixty-five.

"Damn it!" yelled Hellen, hitting the wheel with her hand.

Hyppolite turned to look at her with a smile and said calmly:

> Relax, my darling. Breathe slowly.
> See that radiant sky stretching above us!
> It is covered with pure azure.
> This immaculate blue is its most beautiful outfit.
> Gently it is smiling, asking for your patience.
> Let us return the smile.

Indeed, there was no reason to be frustrated or annoyed. Without the shadow of a cloud, the immaculate sky was glowing from a pure azure, communicating energy to all living beings. The gentle breeze of a lukewarm wind going around, carrying the perfume of fresh soil and wildflowers, was an invitation to breathe deeply and capture the goodness of the open air. In fact, the whole day had been nice. The forecast predicted a sunny day with a remote probability of rain for the middle of the week.

Besides, at that time of the year, seventy-five-degree weather on a Friday evening was a gift handed on a golden platter, a backup for good time, and an accomplice for a perfect and worry-free weekend.

Hyppolite and Hellen usually took turns driving. As they were leaving the highway, they stopped to change seats. Hellen sat behind the wheel. Hyppolite did not stop observing both sides of the road. Sitting at the passenger side, he could not believe his eyes. Everywhere he turned, he saw beauty. Landscapes were vanishing before him, only to discover others even more beautiful. All excited by the close contact with nature, he marveled. To him, each landscape was like a masterpiece parading through his eyes. He stayed quiet for a while, meditating before he turned his eyes to Hellen.

"Everything God does," he said, "he does it right. I think his greatest strength is painting. He does not need palette or tablet to engineer a perfect job. He just does it! He uses the wide-open nature, and every single job is a masterpiece. I think New Jersey is his favorite place to have pampered it with such special touch. It seems that, some parts of the state, the great Creator designed them with his bare hands and personally hung them from the sky."

"You've suddenly become very sensible. Your words are very poetic. I knew you would like it up here."

"How could anybody stay insensible in front of such spectacle?" said Hyppolite with his arm around Hellen's shoulders. "It is not only the beauty. It is also the good spirit it inspires. You feel your heart moving. It's like nature is communicating with you and triggering love and tenderness in you."

"You are right," said Hellen. "They always claimed that Garden State is the best place to fall in love."

"I am from a tropical country," said Hyppolite. "There, the orchards have a time to bloom and produce fruits. The trees keep their green leaves all year-around. But now I am looking at nature, to me, it is a kind of mystery. These trees have a mind of their own. All winter, they went undercover. It is like they went to sleep. The naked branches turned to popsicles under the snow. You would think they were dead. But they were just conceiving more life to resurge stronger than ever as soon as winter is gone. Look at the pleasant surprise, the spectacle they have brought out.

"I compare all this as a pregnant woman. During the gestation period, she is sleepy, not in the mood, sick, slow moving, heavy until she finally gives birth to a healthy baby kicking, yelling, and smiling, a beautiful creature, a fountain of energy, a miracle of life."

"You have a lot more to see," responded Hellen, smiling. "New Jersey is an enchanting place to visit and to live. Indoor or outdoor season, at any time of the year, there is always an opportunity to admire and enjoy a different facet of the state. I have been in a lot of places in and out of the United States. I have had the chance to observe and compare. I can tell you with assurance that New Jersey is a great place. Vacationers usually come from far away to visit it all year-around."

"People from this state must be very happy and proud."

"Yes, indeed. A lot of people usually come out on weekends or for summer vacation, exploring and enjoying their Garden State. But still, the number could be greater, judging by the density of the population. To me, lots of people take for granted the things they should be thankful for and yet proud of. God has doled out to this state natural beauty and prosperity as far as production of goods from the agricultural land. All these things are right here. But because people have them at hand, they do not seem to mind. I mentioned God because, from out here and most part of the Garden State, when in contact with nature, you look up and around you, it is so well designed you know for sure that there is a higher power in control."

"Why did you say people take things for granted?"

"Well," said Hellen, "if, every year, thousands of people spend a great deal of money traveling all over the world for vacation, how do you explain that many of them who live right here in the state don't take necessary time to know it better?"

Anne Marie was looking for a good reason, an excuse that would give her the strength to continue her relationship with Mohammad. To her, he was a good man. He had his character. He had a temper, but he loved her. She had witnessed once when he came down awfully hard on her family, cursing at them, but that did not mean he was the devil. Anybody can have a bad moment. In fact, there is no angel walking around on this earth. Everyone has a bad side and good side. She was already involved with him; she did not feel it was okay to just break that relation, and then what? Another one and another one? No! She remembered Méralie. Her mother always said that it was not decent for a woman to go with a different man every day looking for the right one.

"It's like trying on shoes at the Payless store. Patience is a virtue."

If Mohammad really had a problem, she believed that, with love, understanding, and lots of attention, she would help him overcome whatever was wrong.

Besides, the family's last meeting came in handy and was the perfect pretext for the decision she was about to make. In her own reasoning, if Hyppolite could leave the house to join his life with the woman he loved, why couldn't she do the same thing?

When Hyppolite first came in after the earthquake, she thought, *he had all kinds of problems. Everybody was worried about him. But love has put light in his eyes and life back in his heart. He has changed to become the jovial and handsome man he is now.*

Like a bird ready to fly with its own wings, her mind was made up: she had decided to go with Mohammad. But sneaking out of the house like a thief was out of question. In a conversation with Mohammad, she wanted to know the plan as far as where and how they were going to live. Mohammad pretended that everything was under control, but in his desperation, he was not thinking straight. His first plan was to have the woman he loved at his side. Knowing that would hurt the family was even better. He felt he should be vindicated for being rejected. Meanwhile, Anne Marie was looking all over for her brother, to no avail. She worked during the day; Hyppolite was going to school in the evening and away on weekends. When she finally reached him, it was a Friday evening.

"Hyppolite, where are you? I need to speak to you."

"What's the matter? Are you okay?"

"I just want to speak to you."

"I am not in the city. Since the weather changed, Hellen and I, we have been out on weekends. I never knew the countryside was so beautiful. So far, we have been to Ocean, Cumberland, and Burlington County, visiting the most glorious sights you won't find anywhere else."

"This time of the year," said Anne Marie, "New Jersey is particularly attractive. It's beautiful."

"Yes, indeed. I think we could not have chosen a better time. Just being out here in touch with nature, enjoying those sights, you feel vitalized. It is just like breathing life and energy."

"Where are you now?"

"I am on my way to Princeton."

"You sound overly excited. I am so happy for you, Popo. New Jersey is exceptionally beautiful, but being in love makes you see it as even more fascinating. Enjoy, Popo. Happiness is sometimes ephemeral."

"I will speak to you when I get back. It is true that happiness is ephemeral, but in certain circumstances, you can count on nature. Do you remember this poem of Alphonse de Lamartine?

Quand tout change pour toi
La nature est toujours la même
Et un même soleil se lève sur tes jours

"Meaning,

When everything changes for the worst
The nature is still the same
And the same sun rises on your days

Hellen and Hyppolite fell in love with the Princeton area. They spent all day Saturday going around from the shop galleries to the farmers market, strolling around visiting beautiful gardens, paved terraces, courtyards, and natural woodlands; and they could not get enough of them. In the afternoon, they were at the Prospect House. They marveled at the gardens acclaimed as garden-of-Eden qualities. In front of such spectacle, Hyppolite became emotional. He stayed quiet. His mind was traveling far, and his heart was filled with nostalgia. Standing close to him, Hellen took his hand.

"Don't think too much. Just enjoy the moment. Life does not have to be misery after misery, like a chain of pain and torment. It is true, on this earth, we are not exempted. Anything can happen at any time. But when it becomes too complicated, when we feel overwhelmed, it is often useful just to stand back and remind ourselves of our purpose, our overall goal. When we are faced with feelings of stagnation and confusion, it may be helpful to find a prudent time to simply reflect on what it is that will truly bring us relief and—why not say it?—what it is that will bring us happiness. Based on that, we should then reset our priorities.

"As you're from a tropical country, these orchards and these flowers mean a lot to you. They remind you a great deal of your land. The nostalgia is even greater when you are thinking about that recently catastrophic earthquake. You are human. It is normal that you feel sad. Keep in mind, Haiti will not stay like that. Change will come. The people living there will have to work extremely hard to put it back in shape. It will not be easy. The damage was both material and emotional. It will take time to repair and rebuild, most of all, to heal, to console.

"For the moment, relax and think positive. Remembering the past can reduce your enjoyment, and the anxiety you feel about the future has also the same effect. You need to find a way to put your life back in proper context, allow a fresh perspective, and enable yourself to see which direction to take. Do not forget, if there is life, there is hope. Come on. Look at me. Repeat this serenity prayer with me. 'God, grant me the serenity to accept the things I cannot change, the courage to change the things I can, and wisdom to know the difference.'"

"Thank you," said Hyppolite, hugging her. "Before all that disaster happened to my country, I used to travel very often to my grandmother's property in the countryside. So many times, I witnessed nature in its essence, the wildlife before being affected by bad weather or any other things around it. Now my mind often goes back to those mountains where nature explodes in beauty and goodness. You benefit from the flowers and their perfumes, from the fruits and their shades. I hope the earthquake did not destroy all that."

"No," said Hellen. "The countryside was not much affected. According to the news, the disaster was more severe in the cities where the buildings were not constructed to withstand a 7.0-magnitude earthquake."

-16-

Momentous Decisions

On Monday afternoon, Hyppolite picked up Anne Marie at work and drove to Lincoln Park, where they went for a stroll and talked. Anne Marie was ready to move; most of her belongings were already packed. So far, Mohammad had her clothing and her books. All she was looking for was a kind of encouragement, a booster, to help fulfill her plan and feel less guilty. So who better to talk to than Hyppolite? But it seemed that she was not getting all the support expected.

"Throughout our life, we are all faced with difficult decisions and moral choices," said Hyppolite. "By those momentous decisions, we define ourselves as human beings with the capacity of thinking before acting. I love Hellen with all my heart, but I am not proud of what I did. I should have planned better and informed my mother ahead of time. Sometimes people in love do crazy things. I know that you are in love with Mohammad, but if there is any doubt in your heart, no matter how insignificant, I suggest that you think about it before you cross this line. You need to take time to analyze your feelings, balance the situation, and know if your decision is worth it."

"What do you mean?" asked Anne Marie, a bit disappointed. "What about you? You are living with Hellen. So far, you seem happy."

"Hellen is a self-sufficient, stable, and mature woman. She has been living alone for a long time. She does not need a bodyguard, but I feel like I need to stay by her side, dedicating myself to her. And yes, so far, we are okay. We have decided. We intend to keep it. The future has the last word. But do not take me as an example. Following people without thinking, without trusting your own heart, is not a good idea."

"Tell me the truth. You hate Mohammad, don't you?"

"I do not hate Mohammad. I have thought a lot about his reaction the last time he came to the house, insulting all of us, telling us to go back to Haiti where we belong. To me, it was not possible for someone to burst out like that without any provocation. Something had to trigger such unexpected reaction."

"Are you saying he is crazy or he uses drugs?"

"I do not know. You are my only sister. I love you dearly. You are young, full of illusion. I want you to be happy. A deception can mark you very deeply. I cannot make any decisions for you. Please be careful. Look at the whole picture. Think about the sacrifices you have made through the years to study. At least present your thesis and have your state certification or your degree before you make any decisions. Besides, in this economy, jobs do not grow on trees. You just started working. You were lucky enough to get a job. Now do not blow it. I cannot advise you to drop everything and run after a man without knowing where you stand. Human beings do not live only on love and fresh air. You need to think not only for yourself but also for the children that might come from that relationship."

Anne Marie went back home feeling worse than she did before. When she opened the door, her mother was sitting in the living room with Madeleine, a sister from church who had been her best friend for a long time. They did not see her coming.

"You need to take more care of yourself," said Madeleine, putting a wet towel on Méralie's forehead. "You are dizzy too often. You cannot stand too long on your feet. You have taken your medicine regularly, but still your blood pressure is out of control. I do not know why you do not want to speak to your children. It is important that they know you do not feel good. They would help you. You used to be so joyful, so happy. I do not understand your sudden sadness."

"Ah, Sister Madeleine! Everyone carries their own load. Everyone has their own pain," said Méralie. "Life is so short. It's like a tiny footprint on a storm at seashore. I do not want to be a burden to anyone. My children have their own life. If it is time for me to go, let it be."

"Oh, my dear," said Madeleine, hugging Méralie, "such bitterness of spirit is not at all in your usual character. You are speaking with disappointment and sadness. Only the Almighty God knows when it is time for us to go. Very often, we are stressed out by discontentment, overpowered with heartache and misery. This is part of life because perfect and continuous happiness is not from this earth. God, in his goodness, has put love as a rich and refreshing source of relief to ease our pain and make the life load a bit lighter. Love does not wander. It keeps families united. It opens the door to forgiveness and caring. Your children love you. If they have done something to make you sad, you need to speak out. They are from a different generation, a different era. Maybe, in their foolishness, they do not realize they are hurting you so bad. After all the sacrifices you have consented as a widow, a single mother to raise four children alone, the least they can do now is the best they can to give you peace of mind."

Méralie could hardly speak. With a sadness that came from deep inside, she was trying to keep her composure. Breathing heavily and silently, she closed her eyes, and tears rolled down her cheeks to her shirt. Madeleine ran to the kitchen and brought her a cup of fresh water and tissue to dry her face.

"Since the death of your husband, I have never seen you so sad. You are a woman of faith. You need to overcome this problem."

"I agree. Love is a rich and refreshing source of goodness," she finally said. "But when you get hurt in your love, it is like a low dose of poison that is killing you little by little."

"I do not know what is going on," said Madeleine. "I do not know what is bothering you so much, but something needs to be done. Otherwise, your heart will not resist such pain."

"I have dedicated my whole life to my family," continued Méralie. "When my husband passed, the only thing that kept me going was the love for my children. God had given me a double portion to love them for myself and for their departed father. I guess love has kept me alive. I care dearly for my children. Now I am looking back, I am asking myself how, where, and when I failed. Anne Marie, my only daughter, the baby, I would like to have the best for her. I strain myself to protect her, give her an education, and teach her respect for God and for herself. But since she fell in love with that man, she has become incredulous, rebellious, and defensive. Now my biggest concern is that she is decided to go—God knows where— with this man, a man who hates her family. I am sure he is going to try to hurt her just to get to us."

"Oh, Lord! Have mercy!" said Madeline, surprised. "Anne Marie is young and inexperienced. She doesn't know what she is getting herself into. You need to speak to her. Try opening her eyes before it is too late."

"I am a Christian woman. I always thought that my daughter would leave this house dressed up in white, holding her brothers' arms to the altar. Now what can I say? You bear children but not their character. You can try to teach them good manners, but you cannot lead their life."

"This is the plain truth," Madeleine replied. "A prophet once said, 'Your children are not your children. They are sons and daughters of life longing for itself. They come through you but not from you. And though they are with you yet, they belong not to you. You may give them your love but not your thoughts, for they have their own thoughts. You may house their bodies, not their souls, for their soul dwells in the house of tomorrow, which you cannot visit, not even in your dreams. You may strive to be like them, but seek not to make them like you.'"

"I do not want to restrain my children in anything," continued Méralie. "I would like to see them emancipated, going to places I never dreamed of, getting positions in life I never thought of, but always with discipline and respect. I guess I am a failure as a mother. If Jean Philippe, my late husband, could see what was going on, he would die repeatedly. Now I cannot even go to church anymore. What would I tell the brothers and sisters when they ask for my daughter?"

Still standing in the hallway, Anne Marie was listening to the conversation. She felt cold and hot at the same time. She would like to yield with all her strength and get out that weird feeling that was pressuring her heart, but she could not. Acrimony mixed with pain and fear blocked her throat; she did not make a sound. At that moment, Tertulien, who was coming home from work, opened the door and approached her.

"What is going on? Are you okay? Where is Mommy?"

"Mommy is sick. She is sick," cried Anne Marie as she hurried out the door like a hyper kid scared to get punished for her mess.

She did not want to cry in the streets, but she could not stop the tears that were covering her face. Standing on the sidewalk, she hopped on the 87 bus and sat in the back. She could not stop thinking about the conversation she just heard.

She knew that her mother hardly went out if it was not for an office or doctor visit, always inside the apartment cleaning and cooking for the family. Her only main connection with the outside world was L'Eglise Evangelique Haïtienne de Jesus Christ, the Haitian evangelical church on Kennedy Boulevard. She was usually there on Tuesday and Thursday nights and on Sunday mornings. Anne Marie knew this was her mother's only refuge, her second home, and the place where she met with her friends, the brothers and sisters, to joyfully worship and praise God.

Please, God, she prayed, *help Mommy. Do not let her die. I am scared to get close to her. I do not know what to say.*

Leaning back on the seat, she closed her eyes, trying not to think. Like a refreshing evening breeze coming through your bedroom windows after a rough working day, lots of good memories slowly came through her mind and overshadowed her.

She remembered her father holding her in his arms, dancing with her, while Méralie was sitting in the living room, watching them, smiling and happy. She saw herself sitting on her mother's lap while she was fixing her hair and singing to her the Sunday school songs. How could she forget her mother holding her hand every morning walking her to school, telling her "God loves you. Mommy loves you" before rushing to the courthouse where she was working? She also remembered her mother, much younger, taking them to the park on Sunday afternoon, running around, jumping, and playing ball with them but always very protective and caring for their safety. And last she did not forget that her twenty-first birthday was not long ago. The whole family gathered around her and made her feel so special. Most of all, these words from her brother Hyppolite stayed engraved in her heart: "Tonight there is joy. There is happiness in the air. We gathered to celebrate our sister's birthday, the girl of our heart. It seems that it was yesterday when she came to our life and captivated us all."

She was still dreaming when the bus made its final stop in Hoboken. Getting off with mixed feelings of regret and remorse that brought more tears to her eyes, she stood on the sidewalk and took a deep breath. The harbor smell, mixed with the sweet aroma of chai, a popular Italian tea, made her calm down.

Hoboken always reminded her of the good old days when she used to be close to Benoit, a good friend and perfect gentleman but always in love with her. They were at Dickenson High School. Every Friday evening, instead of going home, they would join their friend Raquel; and together they would walk to one of the parks, sit, and watch as people would come by with their dogs for play or exercise.

Anne Marie was walking, and her memory kept throwing her back to the past. From the cobblestone streets to the house where Frank Sinatra was born, Hoboken had something special that brought back good souvenirs to her. She finally walked to one of the sidewalk restaurants on Washington Street and ordered a coffee. She just wanted to be alone and breathe.

That afternoon, Tertulien took his mother to the doctor; and as soon as he filled the prescription, he called the rest of the family for a meeting. Hyppolite was the first to show up. They were sitting in the living room while waiting for Esaie and Anne Marie.

"I know you've been going away every weekend," said Tertulien. "How do you like Jersey?"

"Growing up in Haiti," Hyppolite said, "I used to go to vacation to the countryside with Grandma. I have always been in love with nature. You feel free. You feel wild, like the wind going through the orchards and competing with the birds of the sky. But since I have been going away on weekends with Hellen, I have noticed things that push me to think. Here, in New Jersey, where man is in complete control of his environment, I get to appreciate another dimension of the nature. The difference is, when good taste and manpower are working along in harmony with nature, it is marvelous. It is glorious. It is beauty wherever you turn. New Jersey is a source of inspiration for any artist. It is a pleasure for any vacationer within or from afar and a pride for its residents. Now I really understand why New Jersey is called Garden State."

"I am happy to hear that. While you have the time, enjoy yourself, brother."

Esaie came home early wondering why Tertulien called him in. The only person missing was Anne Marie, who came in five minutes later with a suspicious attitude. Feeling like a convicted criminal, she entered the living room and sat down quietly, anxious to hear what they were going to say. Tertulien, with a serious tone, did not take time to speak out.

"You must feel very strange," he said, "that, instead of Mommy, I am the one calling for a meeting this evening. For some days, Mommy has been upset, anxious, and unhappy. While working this afternoon, I drove a passenger to Harrison Avenue and took advantage to stop by home. Mommy was pale, dizzy. She could hardly speak, and from what I noticed, she had cried a lot. According to the doctor, she is stressed out. Her blood pressure is uncontrollable, and she is suffering from anxiety. And although she has been taking her medicine, instead of getting better, she is more depressed every day.

"On my way to the drugstore, I could not understand the prescription. The handwriting was unreadable. But now that I have the medicines, I want to bring them to your attention. Our mother never took Prozac or Xanax in her whole life. As far as I know, these diazepam medicines are psychotropic drugs. Our mother is a healthy woman. The most she would take sometimes at night is Sweet Dream, a regular tea that she buys at the grocery store. I am not accusing anybody, but if you know you are doing something to make her upset, please stop it. At least do not bring your bad deed to her attention. I am her eldest child. Since I have known my mother, the only thing she has done is worked and loved her family. After all, she has been through so much to give us an education. She does not deserve to still be worry about us."

"Do not look at me," said Esaie. "I am not the one leaving the house without saying even goodbye, treating her like a stranger."

Hyppolite did not have time to respond.

"Please, Esaie, lower your voice," said Tertulien. "Mother just took her medicine, and she is sleeping. If we are pointing fingers, you should be the first to be targeted, and you know why."

"I resent this accusation," Esaie replied strongly. "I did not push Hyppolite to anything."

"Mommy is not upset with Hyppolite," said Anne Marie. "Instead, she feels relief to see him doing so well. She is grateful to Hellen."

"The other reason I called you is that I would like to take her out for a couple of days. She needs a change of scenery. Since Haiti is not appropriate now, I think, right here in New Jersey, there are a lot of fabulous places that offer fun, exciting, and entertaining attractions we can choose."

"Indeed, this is a great opportunity for outdoor adventure. Why don't we get a location for birding or boating? We can also choose to go camping or relax on the beach."

"I do not think so," replied Tertulien. "Mommy is stressed. She needs a place to relax without too much noise or traffic."

"There are plenty of places we can go," said Hyppolite. "But Mommy needs a place that fits her profile."

"Okay," said Tertulien, "she is sixty-eight years old. She was born in Haiti. She spent her youth in the city going to school, but every summer, she used to go to the countryside, sometimes all the way in the mountains, in full contact with nature. She was twenty-three years old when she came to the United States, and since—"

"Stop!" yelled Anne Marie. "Just stop it! You make it sound like you are reading her obituary. Mommy is not dead yet. She is not dead…Please stop it."

"Please stop crying," said Tertulien with more concern. "Why are you so nervous? When I came in this afternoon, you were standing in the hallway crying. If you know something that we do not know, please tell us."

"Mommy is sick because of me," said Anne Marie, sniffing her tears. "This is my fault. I was listening to her conversation with Madeleine this afternoon. She found out that I was about to leave to go with Mohammad."

"What!" yelled Tertulien and Esaie together.

The news hit the brothers by surprise. It had been a while since they had heard about or seen Mohammad. Esaie and Tertulien thought that man was history in Anne Marie's life.

"How could you!" yelled Esaie. "You yourself witnessed how that man was threatening us. He was not joking. He did what he promised to do. Fortunately, when the police invaded the parking lot and raided the whole building, they did not find anything to accuse us. And we thank God, that Monday, Mommy went to the ladies' meeting at the church with Sister Madeleine."

"I never knew exactly what was going on, why Mohammad would try to set you up, calling the police."

"I think it is time that you know the whole story," said Esaie, upset.

"Keep your voice down please. You do not want to wake Mother up, do you?"

Since Méralie was still sleeping, they went to the van in the parking lot to continue the conversation that got overheated. Anne Marie promised to think better and speak to her family before making an important decision like this.

After a long time debating, everybody moved back inside to speak to Méralie about Anne Marie and tried to save the situation. It was concluded that they were not going to impose a vacation to her. They just wanted her to have an agreeable moment while surrounded by her family. Since she liked nature, a long weekend on a farm that would remind her a bit of her infancy and her homeland would be perfect. So where would be better than right here in the Garden State which had been in favor of "agricultural tourism."

They all agreed that everyone would research a place, and they would vote on it at the end of the week. The meeting was over before Méralie woke up; the rest of the family spent the evening around her, trying to cheer her up.

-17-

A Little Corner of Paradise

When they found out about Méralie's condition, the family pulled around her as one. The boys did their best to be home as much as possible. Anne Marie took over the housework, making sure her mother felt comfortable and took her medication. But as soon as she saw her children around her, Méralie claimed that she was okay. As of the second day, she did not want to stay in bed. Yanique, Esaie's fiancée, was working at Christ Hospital. After work, she got a basket of fruit and nuts at the grocery store and stopped by to visit. As they were in the kitchen chatting, Méralie was cleaning the sink. Suddenly she held on to the counter like she was about to fall.

"Be careful!" yelled Yanique, jumping to her rescue. "Are you okay?"

"I am fine," said Méralie, holding her forehead. "I felt a bit dizzy. For a moment, I went blank."

"Sit down. What did you eat this morning?" said Yanique, who pulled a stethoscope from her bag to check her pressure. "You need to rest. You will have time to do all this cleaning. Come on. You must stay in bed."

"I have so much to do," said Méralie. "I need to cook. Everybody is at work. They will come back hungry later."

Yanique nicely advised Méralie to relax and to get out more often. After caring so much for her children, being mother and father, it came the time when she needed to think about herself. Her health was more important than the housework. Even though she was completely well, she did not have to tire herself like that all day long. The children were grown; she did not have to babysit anybody. She just had to let them cook and take care of her. Some elder sisters from church often sat at the park bench, chatting and getting fresh air; this was a particularly good habit.

"Speaking about church, we have a fundraiser dinner this Sunday. Everybody is bringing something. I already promised that I would bring banana bread."

"Please speak to them," replied Yanique. "You cannot do anything right now."

"This is not easy," said Méralie with a worried face. "I feel like I am failing them. I have already missed two days of church. Last week, I did not attend the Bible study or the prayer meeting. This Sunday, I cannot miss it. You do not know how it feels when people count on you. They are calling you, waiting on you, and you cannot respond.

"I have been thinking about Sister Laurieuse lately," continued Méralie. "That woman was so dynamic, so active, always ready to help. She never said no. When it came to missionary activities, like visiting another church in Brooklyn, attending a revival in Boston or Connecticut—you name it—she was the first to be present. While the church was on the road going somewhere, she was the one leading us in prayers and songs. She was an excellent animator. Last year, she had a stroke. After spending a whole month at Medical Center, she came back home in a wheelchair, and since then, she has never gotten back on her feet. I am telling you. It is sad to see those who began the race of life with so much vigor and potential now sitting on the sidelines watching the parade passing by."

Yanique was touched by the comment. She hugged Méralie while rubbing her back.

"C'est la vie!" she responded. "This is life! But there is a time for everything, a time to run the race of life with all your potential and a time to sit down to watch the parade passing by, for nothing is forever. But if there is life, there is hope. For this reason, you need to follow the doctor's advice. Do only what you can do. Life is not only work and taking care of others. You need to take care of yourself and enjoy life too. Most of all, you need to relax. Remember, your kids care a lot about you. They would like to spend time with you away from these four walls. Please think about that. It would be good for you and for them."

Indeed, the children had been more attentive. They were doing the best they could to shadow her, to make her feel good. But still Méralie had some resentment, for it was not easy to part her from the house, not even for a couple of days. After a while trying to convince her, Hyppolite finally got an answer. With ambivalence, she accepted to spend one day out with them, but she did not seem to agree on any day proposed to her. The following Friday, they dropped everything and took half a day from work; and before she could change her mind, they decided to rush their way out to a resort.

With heartfelt emotion, Méralie's children were looking forward to that quality time with their mother. To them, it was like acquitting a debt, an absolution. She had been taken for granted too long.

No one even remembered how long it had been since the whole family had a picnic or a fun time out. When Esaie and Tertulien were attending Lincoln and Ferris high schools, making thousands of illusions, dreaming of being the athletes of the year, they had time only for their sport activities. Later they started to have interest in the opposite sex; they were thinking more about dating than family reunions. At that time, Méralie, already a widow, was still working, struggling for the daily bread. Between her job and housework, she did not have time for anything else. So breaking away from the daily routine was kind of overdue and well deserved for her, something that should be repeated more often.

That afternoon, the suitcases were already in the car. The boys, standing on the sidewalk and chatting with the neighbors, were just waiting. Anne Marie finally came down with Méralie, and everybody boarded the van. But every time Tertulien started the engine, ready to go, he had to stop. Méralie wanted to get back inside. She forgot something: her slippers left under the bed, her headscarf inside the drawer, her Bible on the night table, etc. Every time someone went up the steps to get something in the apartment, she remembered something else. Finally, they drove off. In case she left anything else, they will get it on the way.

The truth of the matter, Méralie was more worried than mad and more nostalgic and anxious than upset. Since she retired from the courthouse, she never went anywhere. The apartment where she lived, if it were not to attend church services or some rare business trips around Jersey City, she would not leave it at all. As she was devoted completely to her family, her only world was her children. Although they became adults, she never stopped caring for them.

Her only wish, though, was to travel to Haiti, her homeland, so dear and so close to her heart. Haiti was the place she saw the light for the first time, the place of her infancy. Now she was getting up in age, she would have liked to return and stay there for a while. But how would she? She was so attached to her children and her grandson, Joseph. If there were any possibility, instead of going away for the weekend, she would rather make a trip to her homeland. Invaded by a nostalgic sentiment, her strong will was, when the time came to leave this life, she would like to be laid by her parents and grandparents' side.

Sitting in the back of the van with a thousand thoughts running through her mind, she was kind of moody. Tertulien started to worry, wondering if the trip was a good idea. Anyway, no one wanted to push too much; everyone kept quiet. Anne Marie put on some gospel music, hoping for a relaxing moment.

It was 1:45 p.m. when they left. The van turned to Communipaw Avenue and, from US Highway 1 and 9, took Route 280, heading west. The highway was clear; traffic was going smoothly. The afternoon rush hour had not yet started. Being a cabdriver, Tertulien had been on that road so many times. He chose to go slowly, for this was not a business trip.

Méralie did not speak much. But enjoying the gospel music and admiring the landscapes along the way brought her serenity. Speaking to Joseph, her grandson, she started to smile again. Soon she forgot her resentment. The bitterness was gone, and the change did not take time to show: the twinkling of her eyes and the smile on her face brought peace of mind. Everybody was relieved; it was like sipping a fresh cup of water after a long walk under the sun.

Anne Marie, who particularly was carrying a heavy conscience since the day she overheard the conversation between her mother and the lady from church, felt more at peace. Turning her gaze to her mother, she saw an expression of exoneration and tenderness on her face.

Thank God! she thought. *There is nothing more refreshing than forgiveness. This is a kind of generosity and a need for peace that lifts a load right from the heart and gives way for spiritual healing.*

It was around 3:55 p.m. when they arrived at a beautiful and quiet place. Méralie was impressed by her surroundings. She could not stop looking at the bushes, some flowers that she had never seen before. It was like discovering a new world. Since she did not want to go in right away, Anne Marie stayed with her, trying to please her the best she could. The boys, before going inside to check in, grabbed Joseph, who already started to complain about the quietness of the place.

The next day, Méralie woke up early as usual. She woke Anne Marie and wanted to also call the boys.

"It is already six thirty," she said. "They are still in bed. We cannot just sit here without doing anything. People will think that we are lazy. At least you and I can help clean or do whatever needs to be done."

"Just calm down, Mommy," advised Anne Marie. "Everything is paid for. Just say your morning prayers. Relax, and this time, let people serve you."

By nine thirty, no one could keep Méralie inside. Anne Marie and Hyppolite accompanied her for a tour. This resort was one of the places promoting agriculture. The visitors always had a fun activity to do. Guided by a worker from the farm, some people were following with their friends and family, laughing, taking pictures, and picking out their own fruits and vegetables. The bountiful eggplants and green peppers and the copious and giant tomatoes were sparkling like diamonds in the sun. The cherry and apple trees were getting ready for a plentiful harvest. Some fruits, like strawberries, already harvested and piled up in small containers, filled the air with a sweet aroma, pushing you to breathe deeper.

Méralie was walking around with a group. At every step, she got left behind, not because she could not keep up the pace, but because she just could not get enough of her view. She took all her time to observe her surroundings as if she wanted to engrave the whole panorama in her memory. From the bushes carrying flowers so far unknown to her to the giant orchards stretching up willing to kiss the sky, she was like a kid on a carousel. With her arms wide open, she was taking deep breaths like she wanted to store the pure air in her lungs for future use back home, in Jersey City.

Soon the aroma of the ripened fruits broke into her mind, sneaking into her thoughts and refreshing her memory like the morning dew. Slowly she went back in time to her homeland. Under the shade of a tree, she leaned back and stayed a long time with her eyes closed and a smile on her face.

"Thank you, Lord!" she whispered.

Anne Marie and Hyppolite did not want to disturb her in any way. They just stood back looking at her and letting her enjoy whatever thought was the cause of her smile so anticipated. When Méralie finally opened her eyes, she breathed deeply and moved one step forward.

"Are you okay, Mommy?" said Anne Marie, moving closer. "I don't want to see you sad. I feel bad for everything that happened with Mohammad. I promise, whatever important decision I take in the future, I will let you know ahead of time."

"No, no," she said, "I am not sad. On the contrary, going through these gardens have inspired so much peace and serenity. Breathing the fresh air and the aroma of the fruits made me recall my infancy with sudden intensity."

Méralie had been a mom, a counselor, an advisor, and a guide to her family all along, but she was not a storyteller. She hardly spoke about her infancy.

Hyppolite was following with a lot of attention, holding eye contact with her. For being raised with his paternal grandmother, he felt that he had missed a lot from his own mother. He had always been a good listener, but he was particularly interested in what she had to say.

"There are a lot of treasured memories I've never shared with you," said Méralie, who sat under the tree. "I remember, when I was six years old, my mother and I, we used to go for walks in the afternoon. At that time, strolling was part of our daily routine. When the sun was dropping below the tops of the trees, we would walk to a bakery nearby to get bread for the next morning. I remember that blue canvas bag that I would always carry filled with bread. On our way back home, I would take pleasure watching the chickens going into the trees to sleep among the leaves. And I used to ask my mother the same question over and over, 'Why do chickens have to fly into the trees to sleep? They live on the ground, walk around among people, eat and drink on the ground. Why can't they make their bed on the ground to sleep?'

"And my mother would give the same answers over and over, 'Mother chicken often makes her nest on the ground to lay eggs. But when the chickens start to get big, they go in the trees to sleep. Most of all, the rooster must be higher up in the tree, right on schedule, at the crack of the dawn, to crow out to the village. It must let everybody know that it is the beginning of a brand-new day. It is time to wake up. It is time to praise the Lord.' At that time, my parents were living in Jérémie, a quiet and beautiful city of the Grand'Anse Department, located in the south of Haiti.

"When I became an adolescent, we used to spend summers in the countryside, I mean, all the way in the mountains. I made lots of friends then. Well, supported by them, climbing trees, diving in the river, and riding horses were not challenging. Even without the luxury of the big city, life was sweet. That time was the best time of my life. It was the time of adventure, the time when the word *scared* was not part of our vocabulary, the time you would think you would live forever and you were the master of the universe, the time you would fall in love with life.

"Later on, I moved to the United States and settled in New Jersey," continued Méralie. "I was already a grown woman when I was working at the courthouse. To me, it was like yesterday. I never had a car. In the morning, I used to zoom around like lightning in the streets of Jersey City, taking my children to school before going to work. The neighbors compared my sneakers to roller skates! I was so active, so energetic.

"Then came the time when my hair, covered by the ashes of the past, started to turn gray. As time went by, my back started to bow. The arthritis pains become more constant with the frost of so many winters.

"It's like waking from a dream," continued Méralie, changing the tone of her voice. "I have been asking myself, 'When did things change?' Life is not what it used to be. I would say, 'When did ripe become too ripe?' This is a mystery. As we sleepwalk our time through the years, thinking that we are in control of the time, it is passing us by, leaving its prints on us and cascading over us like a waterfall. Now I am here, in this fabulous place that reminds me so much of my youth, I must stop at every step. My aches and pains will not let me go on too fast or too far. I do not know where the good old times have gone. I suddenly realize I have gotten old. Now I understand the true meaning of this song that I often sang with outstretched throat when I was just an adolescent.

> Pendant que je dormais
> Pendant que je rêvais
> Les aiguilles ont tourné
> Il est trop tard
> Mon enfance est si loin
> Il est déjà demain
> Passe, passe le temps
> Il n'y en a plus pour très longtemps

"Meaning,

> While I was sleeping
> While I was dreaming
> The clock's hands had turned
> Now it is too late!
> My infancy is long gone
> Tomorrow is already here
> Time keeps passing and passing
> There is not much left

"Mommy!" said Hyppolite and Anne Marie, touched by Méralie story.

They got closer and hugged her.

"I have already lived my life," said Méralie. "I have lived it fully, happily, and sanely. I had a good childhood with my parents. I was happy with your father, and now I have you. I thank God for all his blessings. I will do my best to continue looking up to the bright side of life. Now my advice to you is to live your life fully and sanely. It is not always easy, but you need to find encouragement, nourish your soul from the good side of life. Everything you do, try to do it with all your heart and with the best intentions. Live one day at a time but live with hope. The Scriptures say:

> Fix your gaze directly before you.
> Make level paths for your feet.
> And take only ways that are firm.
> Do not swerve to the right or to the left.
> Keep your foot from evil.

"One day, you will be able to tell your kids your whole life story without shame or remorse."

Besides Joseph, who was getting on everybody's nerves because he could not communicate with his classmates, the weekend could not be better. Looking at Méralie so happy like nothing ever happened, the children were relieved. Everybody wanted to take credit for coming up with the idea of going away, for choosing the right place, and for making the arrangements. The truth is the trip was indeed agreeable and beneficial to everybody; but the reality was, as long as Méralie had her children with her, she would be happy even in hell.

Hyppolite was particularly relieved by his mother's good mood. Besides, taking advantage of the weekend to rest, breaking out of the daily routine, and leaving behind the tension of the city were beneficial and healthy. But deep inside, he was not completely relaxed. Like a smoker running out of his cigarettes, he felt a bit uncomfortable. He missed something; he was thinking about Hellen. It had been more than four months since he opened his heart to her, and since then, he did not part from her side. With nostalgia, he walked outside to be alone while emailing her.

> Hellen, my dear friend, girl of my heart, love of my love!
>
> I am sitting here in the middle of this beautiful garden with an expanse of the blue skies stretched out above me. This place is marvelous. It is so fresh and so natural; it is a little corner of paradise. Everybody is happy and relaxed, including my mother; she is smiling again. But amid all this beauty and excitement, I glance around and feel emptiness that hurts. Suddenly the flowers have lost their color and their charm: you are not here.
>
> Hellen, you are the reason for my joy and happiness. You fill up my senses like the freshness of the morning. You are in my heart, you are in my dreams, and you are on my mind. I am sorry that you are not physically here with me. I realize that I cannot live without you. I cannot wait until tomorrow to see you again and be at your side.
>
> I love you,
> Hyppolite

But his solitude was not too long. Tertulien and Esaie, walking around, noticed him sitting under a tree and joined him.

"What are you doing here alone?" asked Tertulien, just to tease him. "Are you nostalgic? Are you dreaming about Hellen?"

Hyppolite turned around; he was about to say something when Esaie intervened with a more serious matter.

"Messieurs, I've wanted to speak to both of you for a while now. Something has been bothering me. Since you always think that I am a womanizer, I have not said anything before, but it is about Takeema."

"What?" said Hyppolite. "Are you still thinking about this woman? Isn't Yanique enough for you?"

"Listen to me!" yelled Esaie. "This is serious. Takeema was living across the street. As you know, she was stalking me day and night. Suddenly she disappeared without a trace. Last week, her cousin came from Newark looking for her. She told me that Takeema's belongings are still scattered all over the apartment, and no one in the neighborhood, even the man she was living with, seem to know her whereabouts."

"What do you think happened?" asked Hyppolite.

"I don't know," responded Esaie. "But I am very worried."

"Stay out of this," said Tertulien. "This is the only advice I can give you. You had something with this woman. It was long time ago. No one knew about it. It's better that you keep it that way."

While the boys were talking, Anne Marie took advantage that Méralie fell asleep to come out and join them. Since she knew Takeema, the men did not hesitate to share their new preoccupation with her.

"Did you try to get any information? Did you speak to anyone in the neighborhood? Maybe someone knows something about her."

"I didn't dare speak to her boyfriend. That man is crazy. I don't want any problems."

Anne Marie stayed quiet for a while. The expression on her face suddenly changed.

Looking at Esaie, she commented, "You said Mohammad had something to do with the police coming to the building, looking for compromising evidence. I hope you are not thinking that he had his hand in this."

"You still care about this man," said Esaie. "No one even mentioned his name."

"I don't know," intervened Hyppolite. "I don't think Mohammad had anything to do with this. But I saw him the other day speaking to Edmond on the corner of Communipaw and Jewett. Both looked suspicious. I think he is dragging this boy on a bad path."

Anne Marie did not seem so happy with the conversation. She remembered meeting Edmond in the street twice, and both times, he had said he was going somewhere for Mohammad, but he never specified exactly. Anne Marie got up and went back inside.

"So what do you think happened to Takeema?" said Tertulien.

"Men, we are here with family. It's time to relax and have a good time," said Hyppolite. "Let's not spoil the moment or the environment with any worrisome conversation. Let us just pray that Takeema is okay."

Part 4
Another Opportunity

What is more beautiful, more plentiful,
more intense than the youth?
But time is of the essence.
A beautiful life is not related to luck.
It's a goal well planned while young
that carries out in the adult age.

My Son

My son, life is keeping you down
Pain and misery are all that you own
As much as you want to break out of the bond
Crying for help, you don't utter a sound
Like prey overpowered by a ferocious animal
You are looking down fearing the blow fatal
But if along the way another opportunity shows up
Please don't think twice; do not wait up
For your own sake, hold it fast
Grab it as if it was the very last
For it is more capricious than life itself

-18-

Summer Vacation

Méralie was a Haitian woman from the old school. She was a Christian lady who was brought up with respect and consideration for others. As well, she had tried hard to raise her children with almost the same concept. According to her, it is good to apply all your will to the pursuit of a goal and achieve it. This is part of being human, a responsible citizen, and a member of society. But life is not a race where you are pressing forward and get whatever you want no matter the price to pay or who you knock down on your track; there are rules and regulations to follow. Besides, it is always good to pause even for a second, take a retrospective look at your life, and think of what you have done in terms of your relationship with people surrounding you and with God.

The family did not go to a spiritual retreat; but spending a whole weekend in a different setting, away from the pressures of the city and the daily exigencies of life, was quite beneficial. Not only was it good for a physical rest, but it had also served to meditate and to be in touch with themselves.

They came back refreshed and anew with the resolution to watch out and support one another. As for Méralie, the change was surprising. There is no need to be a psychologist to notice that the stress and the pressure was gone. Like an iceberg lettuce that had been sitting in water, she was happy. Her face was illuminated with a joy from within.

All the good intentions and propositions to live as a good citizen and a Christian were there, but how can you survive in an upside-down world where people are doing just the opposite? How do you walk on a straight path, minding your own business without being bothered, when the crude reality is always knocking at your door?

On Sunday evening, the family came back home. As soon as the van pulled in front of the building, Anne Marie went straight to the mailbox to pick up the correspondence. On her way upstairs, she sat on the steps to read a note addressed to her; it was from Mohammad. As she was going through it, she was shocked; Mohammad became meaner and meaner. The loving and charming young man who used to say things so sweet and so romantic seemed to be long gone.

Anne Marie woke up bright and early on Monday. She made sure that Joseph was set for the day; he would not come back home too early because of track practice. She was moving around the house, getting ready for work, but her mind was moving faster. She was thinking about all that was said last weekend. She was thinking about Mohammad and started nourishing ambivalent feelings. She did not completely change her mind about moving with him, but because of Méralie's signs of depression, she was thinking of postponing it.

Now, putting her thoughts together, she was wondering if her brothers were completely right. At first, all these insinuations about drugs sounded like false accusation, but the more she thought about it, the more doubt and uncertainty set in her mind. She had tried to cut the relationship, but he had sworn to control his temper. Although her family disapproved, they got back together. Why had he changed so much? This was not the man she knew. She finally decided to have a serious talk with him. For her family and the sake of their love, she did not want to be overcome by emotion, rushing things. Time is the best counselor of all.

She left early to work that morning, and by seven forty-eight, she was in the parking lot. Going up the steps with her bag and pocketbook on her shoulder, she took her time, greeting and waving to coworkers crossing her way. At the checkpoint, right before entering the building, she found Mohammad waiting and demanding to speak to her.

The building she worked at was a huge facility, a monster edifice that sheltered other government programs. Eight o'clock in the morning was time for heavy traffic. Employees and visitors were rushing in like an overflow river. This unexpected visit of Mohammad was not an agreeable surprise, for it was neither the time nor the place for such meeting. Anne Marie went back outside for a couple of minutes just to hear what he had to say. As she stopped to face him, his demeanor spoke louder than his mouth; he did not show any sign of tenderness. He claimed that Anne Marie went away with her family when she was supposed to be moving with him. And while she was out, she did not call him or answer her phone. The way it was, it seemed that she was playing with him. They spoke just for a couple of minutes; Anne Marie could not convince him at all. It was getting late to sign in. As she ran into the elevator to get to her floor, a security approached her discreetly.

"Are you okay?"

"Yes, I am okay," responded Anne Marie, a bit shaky and embarrassed.

"If you feel like you are being bullied or intimidated, please let us know. Be careful."

Since Joseph came to live with his father, Méralie was in a more active and pleasant mood. She had been encouraging him, talking faith to him, and helping him the best she could with homework. When it was possible, she would take him with her to the evening service. Like a typical Haitian woman would say, the boy became her cane, the strength of her old days.

Now that the cold weather was gone, you would not find her in bed. She was always on her feet, moving in the house, humming her gospel songs, and getting things done. Once the coffee was ready, she would sit by the kitchen table reading her Bible, waiting for Joseph to come out for breakfast before going to school. To her, every minute and every second spent with her grandson would serve to compensate for lost time. When her husband passed away, the children were still young. As she became father and mother, she had to work overtime to cover the house expenses; she could not dedicate them much time. Now that she had retired, she proposed to keep Joseph close as much as she could.

What's more beautiful, more plentiful, more intense than the youth? she thought. *This is the time for learning, spiritual progress, social promotion, developing the talents. The knowledge and experience they store at this age would lead them to be the citizens of the future, to be members of their family and their community. A beautiful life is not related to race or just luck. It is the goal well planned while young that carries out in the adult age. But the youth do not have enough maturity to understand all that. They need the wisdom of the elders to help them launch a brighter tomorrow.*

One afternoon, Méralie was getting ready to go to Ferris High School for Joseph's report card. Tertulien and Anne Marie were at work. She would take advantage to speak to the teacher. Hyppolite came to pick her up, but at her insistence, he dropped her at the corner of Baldwin Avenue and Montgomery Street. Since she was in the habit of walking, she wanted to continue her own.

That Friday afternoon was bright and warm under the immaculate sky of June. Hyppolite, on his way to Bayonne, had to slow down; the traffic was overwhelmed with people crossing the intersections and standing on the sidewalk, moving in all directions. With his foot kept on the break, he was gazing around and wondering why so much commotion. As the traffic got heavier, cars and buses detoured to Kennedy Boulevard and Martin Luther King Drive to avoid the standstill at Bergen Avenue. From Claremont to Audubon Avenue, the whole area was completely closed to traffic. The front of Snyder High School was flooded with people: mothers walking around holding their children's hands with a gratifying face, students proudly wearing their blue gowns throwing their caps in the air, and some others much younger running after other kids, yelling and laughing with a sensation of liberty that shot up their energy sky high; it was pure joy and happiness. As a matter of fact, the whole city of Jersey City was in high gear; for in most of the streets, the same scenario was being displayed. At Dickinson, Ferris, and Lincoln high schools and the vocational and elementary schools, parents and friends dressed in their best were gathering inside and around the schools waiting to receive report cards and attending the graduation ceremonies of their children.

The end of the school year busts the door wide open on the summer season, the return of freedom and a well-deserved break. After ten months of hard work and sacrifice—waking up early morning, studying, and spending hours doing homework—there comes summer vacation: the season of outdoor activities and running free and the time for joy, love, and friendship. Some students go away to different parts of the state enjoying the goodness of nature, visiting relatives, and getting closer to the wildlife.

The ones who do not have the means to go away will also enjoy their vacation. Because when it comes to passing time, Jersey City has it all to make your life easier and more agreeable in terms of recreation. They have lots of programs for kids and teenagers. From sports to homework help, the Department of Recreation offers a variety of programs for the youth to help them stay physically and mentally fit.

Thank God for these programs, Méralie thought.

Anne Marie was quick and vigilant; she already made all necessary steps to enroll Joseph in the summer basketball camp; the family did not have to worry about it.

Indeed, Anne Marie had always been attentive and ready to advise or even get the right information to help others. But as they often say, "A knife cannot scrap its own handle." This saying fits perfectly; for when it came to herself, she was uncertain, hesitant, and unclear.

Lately she had been nervous. Under Mohammad's constant pressure, she kept putting off leaving Jersey City, giving excuse after excuse. She was in love, but at the same time, doubt and fear were setting in. As the days were passing by, Mohammad's patience was wearing very thin. The story she needed to complete her work with Hudson Community College did not stick anymore. She did not have any idea how to get out of this. Sooner or later, she would have to make the sacrifice, for she already gave her word.

Now her goal was to make sure her mother did not get depressed like the last time. She understood that it was very depriving to stay home alone the whole day, thinking about all kinds of problems. It would be better for her to get out more often and be active in the community. But knowing her well, she thought it was not easy to just approach her with the conversation; she had to wait for the right time.

Coming home tired one evening, Anne Marie went to the kitchen, where her mother was waiting. Sitting by the table with her glasses sitting out down on her nose, Méralie was outlining a plan for the next ladies' meeting. She needed information about Joseph's summer activities. Anne Marie briefly gave her the name, the schedule, and the location of the camp and rapidly jumped on the opportunity to introduce her to a variety of programs for senior citizens.

"In Jersey City," she said, "there are plenty of programs rich in leisure, culture, and physical fitness for the residents of the community. The Department of Recreation ensures the utilization of the city's recreational facilities, both indoor and outdoor, encouraging people of all ages to partake in activities that rejuvenate the body as well as the mind. Since you are fluent in English, you will be able to communicate and actively participate in whatever program. Besides, being sixty-eight years old is not old. So far, you are in good health. This is the perfect time to enjoy life wisely and plentifully."

But it seemed Méralie was not too comfortable with the idea.

"There is so much to do to keep a house going. I do not want any entertainment outside. With all of you running around inside leaving your trail behind, I barely have time to keep the house cleaned. If I have free time, it is for my Bible reading and my meditation. Besides, every other evening, I join the prayer or the ladies' meetings. That is enough."

As Anne Marie insisted, Méralie paused a minute; and with haughty and defiant severity, she raised her head and looked straight at her.

"People nowadays," she said, "they look at themselves in the mirror. They feel so great. They talk about the glories of youth, but they don't realize how ephemeral that is. To me, a couple of wrinkles in the face and graying hair should be considered as a blessing instead."

Anne Marie was so surprised at her mother's reaction that she stopped the conversation short.

The truth was that Méralie had her own well-established agenda in secret. She proposed to bring together the ladies of her age living in the neighborhood and expose a problem existing in the community that has occupied her thinking for some time. The plan was to address young people who have dropped out of school for the streets, motivate them, and educate their families to help them recover

A lot of parents nowadays are always on the go, she thought. *They don't take time to be with their kids. They are raising them on the diet of television, in the filth of profanity. Late at night, kids are playing in the park with friends without an adult's surveillance. We are living in a dangerous time. We cannot just sit on our front porch, keeping our mouths shut and watching some of our youths messing with drugs and alcohol and going down.*

-19-

A Bitter Taste of Fear

At Méralie's home, things seemed to be working out simply fine. Apparently Anne Marie was doing well. She had a good job. She was studying still and was getting ready to turn in her last project. Joseph, the youngest member of the family, was coming along as well. The family had bent together firmly but with love and attention around him. His best friend, Raymond, came over more often. Instead of hanging in front of the building, Méralie preferred them watching TV inside. Discreetly she would be able to keep a better eye on them.

As for Méralie, despite her family's disagreement, she continued speaking to the neighbors, giving advice. Every morning, around ten o'clock, she usually walked to the bodega at the corner to get anything that was missing for dinner. The children worried. They insisted that she call them at work so that they would stop at the supermarket on their way home, but she became more stubborn every day. Now she even found better excuses to go out. Since Joseph came to live with the family, she claimed that she needed fresh milk every day. Young children need more vitamin D for their health.

The reality is, even when there was not any excuse at all, she would invent one. For the sake of the community, she proposed speaking to other retired ladies living in the neighborhood and exposing the problems that were going on with some adolescents who might have needed help. The plan was to raise awareness on getting parents' attention for the well-being of their children.

Like a Jehovah's Witness, she would be on her feet walking long blocks, offering people some family advice and a *Daily Bread* booklet. She was known in the neighborhood. Some people would pay attention while some others just dismissed her with a wave of their arm. But the worst you could do was to tell her to slow down because of her age. Méralie did not regret being older, but she did not want to feel incapacitated by people's opinion. Her saying was "Whether young or old, people get sick and die at any time."

It was true she missed the agility of running out, taking care of business in a flash, and having time to come back before the children came home. She missed the strength and the energy of bounding up the stairs and carrying more than one bag of groceries at a time. She missed the Sunday afternoons when she used to walk with her children to the park, running around, jumping, and playing ball with them.

She had gladly exchanged them with the experience and wisdom she had, and those only came with age. It is fair to say she graciously carried her sixty-eight years. She kept her smile, her loveliness, and her ingenuity. She could be stressed out for a moment. But just a word of comfort, a hug from her children, and a prayer from a sister, she would regain confidence; and she would be smiling again. It was like the goodness and the trust of her young age stayed captive in her personality. As long as she was on her feet, able to do something to help; she would not stop.

When it came to Hyppolite, he did not like to speak much about himself or other people. Well reserved, almost quasi timid, he would pass unnoticed to anyone. But when you get closer, you would discover a pleasant human being with a good sense of humor. Dedicated to his business activities as well as his studies, he was of those who never stop striving to "be all that they can be." It is not extreme to compare him to "a good book with an insignificant cover." Just start turning the pages; you will find grace and a mind of knowledge.

Although Hyppolite always dropped by the house to check on his mother while passing by, he and Hellen often visited the family on weekends. That weekend, he called to make sure everybody was home; he had an announcement to make. Méralie, on her feet and happy, prepared the family's favorite meal. Regardless of what her son had to say, just the fact she would be surrounded by all her children, her joy was complete. Esaie had to meet Yanique that Sunday, but Hyppolite wanted the whole family to be home. This announcement was particularly important.

At the dinner table, Hyppolite meticulously chose his words to speak up.

"I give thanks every day for the family that I have. I remember, not too long ago, I was full of fear and no hope at all. Although I was desperately begging for a job, deep down, I had doubt that I was good for something. I thought I would never get back on my feet. I will never forget your support and your love toward me. I thank God for my mother, who never stops inspiring me with courage and hope. You guys, I would not have made it without you. I finally realize that fear is the worst thing that can happen to a human being. It is a blinder that keeps you prisoner and stops you from reaching out for the opportunity of your life. Now I understand that nothing is over until you stop breathing. But you need to have the courage to believe in your potential and hold on to your dream.

"I bring great news today. I have been working very hard, putting in extra hours. With dedication, focus, and sacrifices, the van is now paid off. We can say we are off the hook. Also, I have completed some classes at Hudson Community College. I still have a long way to go, but this week, I just received a state certification for business administration. My plan is to expand the delivery business. I would like to have your opinion on this. To reach a goal, we need to keep working toward it. As much I can, I must keep pressing on, continuing the daily struggle."

Surprised by the unexpected news, the family stayed quiet for a minute, looking one at the other.

Suddenly Esaie broke the silence in an explosive shout, "Bon Dieu Bon!"

"All the time!" exclaimed Tertulien.

"All the time!"

"Bon Dieu Bon!" the others shouted.

Everybody was hugging Hyppolite and hugging each other. Méralie could not be happier; tears of joy ran down her cheeks. Too excited, she could not stay in one place. As she went to the kitchen to grab something, Hyppolite, lowering his voice, took advantage to disclose more news.

"It also seems that Hellen is expecting."

As everybody was celebrating, Esaie, in his perspicacity, asked Hyppolite to step outside; and Tertulien instinctively followed them to the van.

"I have been observing you," said Esaie, "and I feel something is not right. You have the entire recipe to be happy. Why are you so nervous? Is it Hellen? You have said many times that you two are getting along fine. Now, if you are about to have a child, you should be happy. What is holding you back?"

"Hellen is an angel that fell right from heaven and landed into my life. I have no complaints. But you know life itself is a challenge. The road is long, not easy to navigate. God willing, we will get somewhere. So far, I am walking the walk. But *tonerre!* No matter how clear the horizon is, the shadow of the past seems to follow, bringing an aftertaste of fear, trying to rob the peace!"

Touched by the statement, Tertulien stayed quiet for a while before he replied, "Popo, the terrible catastrophe that happened was painful for everybody. I understand you were directly affected. You were right there. But you need to overcome that nightmare. You cannot dwell on it forever."

"The earthquake, I will never forget it, even I live to be hundred years," said Hyppolite. "It is stamped indelibly in the recesses of my heart, but my preoccupation is something else. It is not only for me but for this baby that is coming. Will I be around to raise him? Would he be proud of his father? So far, there are questions without answers, principally the one that concerns us."

"I don't understand," said Esaie, getting nervous. "Please make up your mind. Speak clearly to us. What is going on?"

"Hyppolite," intervened Tertulien in a more serious tone, "perfect happiness is not from this earth. Challenges sometimes come on the way. They are nothing but pure frustration. It is life! Now that you have a plan to improve your situation, you need to take one day at a time. If you are trying to dig too deep, you will find yourself inside the hole."

"We have a pending issue that never got any answer," said Hyppolite. "To me, it is like a time bomb that is waiting to explode."

The brothers kept quiet, looking at each other like they knew what he was talking about, but no one dared pronounce the word.

"The package!" Tertulien yelled suddenly, breaking the silence. "Where is the package? Is that what you are talking about?"

"Now, not even Takeema is around to tell us anything," said Esaie. "I am sure that she knew something."

"Please don't bring her in the conversation. Thank God that woman is gone!"

"Don't you realize that Takeema disappeared the same day the package went missing?" screamed Esaie, upset. "I feel something is not right. Why did no one ever say anything about this awful package? Why has Takeema never called? Knowing her the way I knew her, wherever she was, she would have called, even if it was just to bother me."

"You have me even worried," said Hyppolite.

"We are all powerless," said Tertulien. "No one knows what happened. To tell you the truth, it is better this way because now, even if I knew where it was, I would not look for it. The only thing we can do is change our attitude toward the whole situation. We do not have to think about that and feel miserable. You, Popo, look on the bright side of life and continue your way, making the best of whatever you are doing. Case closed."

-20-

Better Off Alone

Mohammad, for some reason no one knew about, became under pressure and wanted to get out of Jersey. He would like to disappear immediately and come back later for Anne Marie. Thinking, if she stayed close to her family, she would break up with him, he vowed not to leave her behind. Counting on her love for him and her fear of scandal, he was using all kinds of intimidation to gain power and maintain control over her. He became more and more demanding. It was like a fire he needed to light under her to get her to take off with him faster.

Anne Marie was aware of Mohammad's temper; but for the sake of love, she was controlling the situation and managing the tension, hoping he would get back to normal. As he became more belligerent, she had to make a conscious effort to keep him quiet. So she put on a happy face. She did not mention what bothered her in the relationship, nor did she disclose the truth or request any assistance from anybody else.

But how much could she stand? There is a limit for everything; even metal, when submitted to extreme heat, reaches a breaking point. Indeed, the pressure started to take a toll on her. In the office, she could not focus like before. Her heart raced at the thought that he could be waiting at the exit.

One Friday morning, she was at the office early. Mohammad started calling every half hour. He urgently wanted to see her; he would be waiting by the gate in the afternoon. Meanwhile, he kept sending text after text:

> This relationship is going to hell.

> You do not want to go out anymore, not even to a restaurant or a movie.

> It is like you are trying to avoid me.

> I know the problem, and I am ready to correct it as soon as possible.

> You fear your family.

> I went to City Hall this morning and got the necessary information. We must go there and apply for a marriage license. While we are there, we will check to see if a judge is available for the ceremony. If not, we can schedule an appointment for later this week. I love you.

> Nobody is going to keep you away from me. We have to leave Jersey City right after.

Anne Marie had her back to the wall. She felt like Mohammad was dominated by hatred—a burning, venomous hatred—in his heart against her family. How could he decide like that without even asking her opinion? Sitting in the office with her head pounding, she did not even eat lunch. She wanted to clock out and go to bed, but she could not face her mother.

That day, Méralie was not home. She usually made her tour around ten o'clock in the neighborhood. She would walk down Martin Luther King Drive. Slowly she would turn at Clendenny Avenue, go past Bergen to Kennedy Boulevard, continue a couple of blocks, and turn back up. She particularly enjoyed walking down

Harrison Avenue. She would stop under those huge shade trees, enjoying the morning freshness, and lecture anyone who gave her a couple of minutes. Whether it was a young man standing at the corner or a young lady with a can of beer, she always had a word of wisdom or a quote from the Gospel to share.

"No, my sister. Hold his hand and speak to him softly," she told a young mother who was yelling at her kid. "Explain why he cannot run in the middle of the street. Show him love. He will understand. Love makes children grow with more grace. It makes them more confident. From the very beginning, your love for your children affects how they develop. Whatever you do or say in front of these little ones, they will repeat the same thing."

The woman, a bit upset with the child, said thank you and continued her way, holding his hand.

Méralie was on her way back home when she met Louissaint, the son of her neighbor, a young man who just came back from prison. She had the opportunity to speak to him before. He had been arrested in the past, and every time he came back home, he always promised to be serious and quit any wrongdoing. Indeed, he would be diligently looking for job but to no avail. The job situation was hard, and his record made it even harder to succeed. He was coming out of the liquor store with a bottle wrapped in a brown paper bag when he met Méralie.

"My son," she said, "I have known you since you were a little boy. Your mother and I, we are still friends. You are a brilliant man. You have gone through a lot. You have frustration, and you have suffered, but what you are doing will not help. On the contrary, you are putting yourself in more trouble. You have tried alcohol, drugs, gambling, and so forth. These things will not fill the emptiness of your heart. They will not quiet the cry in your soul. You will be thirsty and hungry still. You are not a bad person. I can see that in your demeanor."

"Godmother, I wish you knew what I am going through. While I was in jail, I learned a profession. I am good at it, but no one wants to give me a chance. What do you want me to do?"

"You do not have to continue this way, living in torment with every nerve in your body crying for a fix, for a drink. You are God's creature. Why don't you come to the prayer meeting with me? There is a revival starting tonight. God is wonderful. He loves you. He will help you. He will guide you. He will still love you when you are down. He will wash you with his precious blood until every stain is gone."

Louissaint had heard those words before, when he was younger. He used to go to church with his mother. He stayed quiet for a while listening to Méralie. No one knew what was going on in his mind as he stood there with his hands in his pockets, his jaw muscles moving and his eyes filled with tears. Suddenly he shook his head, turned around, and ran away.

"What are you doing, Mommy?" said Hyppolite, getting close to Méralie. "Let us go home! I am worried. "It is not safe to be out all the time talking to people. When you get to a certain age, a lot of factors come in to play. There are things your health and your strength will not let you do. People have different kinds of problems. How much can you do?"

"I know I am getting old. My hair is turning gray," said Méralie, annoyed. "People grow old. They retire from their regular job, but that doesn't mean they have to stop pursuing their dreams. There is no need to be sitting home, watching TV all day long with a jar of candy at their side. If my feet can take me wherever I want and as long as my mind is functioning, I want to be an asset for my community."

Anne Marie was still in the office. Usually the employees, once their shift ended, did not delay a minute inside the building. Always on the run, the most robust, instead of waiting for the elevators, sieged the stairs.

At exactly three forty-five, like a torrent that finally breaks its dikes, a stream of workers rushed to the exit door, invaded the parking lot, and disappeared into the streets, toward freedom. So taking advantage of the hustle and bustle of the departure, Anne Marie left her car in the parking lot of the office and walked out by another exit.

The sun, still high in the sky, brightened the afternoon and added the last touches to a beautiful day. Most of the public offices were already closed. Some banks, as a courtesy to the working population, stayed late on Thursdays and Fridays. Around Journal Square, the combination of the dry air and the fresh breeze infused a kind of energy, a feeling of freedom and socialization to all. The young people who were window-shopping and strolling around, instead of going home, flooded the restaurants and the ice-cream parlors. After all, "thank God it's Friday!"

Mohammad had to meet with some friends later in a nearby location. He kept on calling Anne Marie, thinking they would meet at Popeyes to put the last touch to their plans; Anne Marie did not answer the phone.

Intimidated and nervous, she walked around the whole afternoon, trying to clear her mind before going home. She did not want to face anybody in the house or hear them mention Mohammad's name. From Academy Street, she turned to Bergen Avenue, kept walking, passed Gifford Avenue, and continued until the corner of Audubon and Wegman Parkway, where she realized she had left her house way behind.

It was getting late. The sun was already gone on the horizon, gradually giving way to the first shadows of the evening. Anne Marie could not feel her feet. Tired, she sat on a bench in the park, gathering her strength and her thoughts. On the other side of the street, she was looking at Raymond, the boy from her neighborhood, standing at the bus stop. Since she was not in the mood for conversation, she stayed quiet.

As it started to get dark, she got up to go back home. Suddenly the boy ran across to speak to someone who was waiting at the other end of the park. Instinctively she followed him only to discover that Mohammad was yelling and threatening to kill the boy for not following his instructions. Immediately a thousand thoughts came to her mind: Who was Mohammad? Was he a drug trafficker? What was the relationship between him and this teenager who was friend of Joseph, her nephew?

Trembling with emotion, she could not explain the precise meaning of this meeting at the park, nor could she understand the sudden pain that gripped her stomach and made her want to throw up. Without listening to the end of the conversation, she moved back. Instead of going home, she caught a bus and called her old friend Raquel.

Anne Marie was on her way to the food court of Newport Mall. On a simple sight, it was noted that she was not the same happy, joyful girl who used to walk leaping on tiptoe, showing her white teeth through her beautiful smile. Sad, fearful, and with a routing behavior, she tried to hide behind the pair of shades covering her face.

Raquel was sitting all the way in the back. As she got up to welcome her friend, she pushed her out at arm's length, pulled the glasses off, and looked at her straight in the eyes. Anne Marie was trembling, with her face wet with tears. Without asking her any question, she gave her a big hug and ordered two ice teas, and they both sat down.

"What is up with the thesis?" asked Raquel, finally breaking the silence.

"I have not started anything yet," said Anne Marie. "The ideas are there, but I cannot find the time to concentrate."

"Don't you have a deadline?"

"I must turn the papers in by the end of August, before school starts again."

"I never knew you as someone to delay work. You have been so intelligent and always ready to jump on a project. You need to get your priorities in order. Get it together, my friend!"

Anne Marie bowed her head down, like she felt uncomfortable to speak. "It is okay. I am working on it."

"You are not okay," responded Raquel. "What happened to you? Why are you so sad? Is it Mohammad? What did he do to you?"

Anne Marie, trying to hide her face, began to speak, "I am in a dilemma. He became so possessive, so arrogant, and even abusive. The other day, he came to my job early in the morning with alcohol on his breath. He does not want to hear any reason. Only his words matter. I told him we need to talk. I asked him to go to Liberty Park, where we would have plenty of time to speak. He told me he is not an idiot romantic like my brother Hyppolite, who sees marvel anywhere he goes. He was not going to sit there, staring at the water under the sun, and think they are drops of pearls and diamonds. He is a busy man. On two occasions, I saw him speaking very suspiciously to some people. I did not interrupt him, but when I confronted him about that, he simply said that I am a woman and I am not supposed to know everything."

"Before we go on, I would like to ask you a question," said Raquel, pissed off by the conversation. "Did you marry him?"

"No."

"I cannot tell you exactly what to do," continued Raquel. "You are the only one who gets to decide if you are happy or not. I am not walking in your shoes. I do not know how much love you have in your heart for this man, but I feel bad to see you crying like this. Things happen in our life to make us sad, even depressed. Sometimes the day seems long and dark without a ray of light. But remember, at any point in time, you have the power to control your life. Do not let any outside force decide for you. Do not put your happiness in the hands of other people. You do not have to live somewhere that does not make you happy or stay in a relationship just because you are scared. Do not sacrifice yourself to please others.

"The devil is a liar. If Mohammad suddenly changed into a bully, he was never a good man. He was only faking. Now he is showing his teeth because of your family's rejection. Thank God it is now rather than later. So far, you do not have any legal commitment to him. Otherwise, it would be worse.

"Do not run through life so fast that you forget where you have been. You also need to plan carefully and know where you are going. You are too young for all of this. Life is not a race but a journey to be enjoyed every step of the way. If he is acting out now, what would happen if you married him and had children? You must decide yourself what to do. It is nice to be respectful, but do not let people take you for granted. You are a very smart young woman. Do not let this man take away your beauty, your loveliness, your charm. Do not let heartache turn your beautiful smile to a grimace. The moment you notice yourself falling out of love with life, you must step back and reevaluate what decision you have made thus far.

"You are a child of God. Do not let anybody destroy you. It is hard to break away from someone that is pulling you down, but that pain is less than reaching your dream. One of the saddest things is to get to the end of your life and wonder, 'What would I have become? What could I have accomplished if I do not listen to him?' I think it's okay to say 'Stop. No more.'"

During all that time, Hyppolite was in the house. He dropped everything he was doing to keep his mother company while waiting for the others to come home. So far, he could not convince her to lessen her approach to people in the neighborhood.

"As I walk down the streets," said Méralie, "my heart breaks. I look around, and a rage builds up in me. There is something going on that is so mind boggling, so heartbreaking, that it begs for a description. This week alone, going to church, I spotted three memorials. I tried to cross to the other side and just pass by like nothing happened, but I could not help it. I had to stop for a moment. I do not know these people. Maybe I never saw them, but as I looked at the picture of these young faces printed on the T-shirts, I feel a pain coming from the pit of my stomach like a woman in labor. The worst part of it is that it seems that the public is immune. For seeing so much, people become numb. They stay quiet, and the situation becomes a new norm."

"A lot of people you see in the streets," said Hyppolite, hesitating, "they are not what you think. They are not angels."

"I know they are off course, they are broken, and they make poor decisions. It is easy to judge. It is their own fault. But if it was not for the grace of God, that could be us. Instead of looking down at people, pointing your finger, you should know better. They do not need more condemnation. A lot of people are hurting. They may not have the advantage that you have. They never felt the love, the approval that you found. They were not raised by parents who invested in them. You do not know what you would be if you had to walk in their shoes. If you want my opinion, the longer I live, the less judgmental I become. Instead of condemning, why don't we try to help heal?"

Esaie and Tertulien came in, but no one was able to make Méralie change her mind. When Anne Marie finally made it home, she just mentioned that Raymond was not allowed in the house anymore and went straight to her room.

Hyppolite proposed that they find out if there were any kind of youth program where retired people like Méralie would get involve as volunteer. Meanwhile, she should at least get coverage from the church. If the pastor agreed, it would be under the umbrella of evangelization, and other ladies would accompany her while doing outreach.

Méralie was finally relieved. With a smile on her face, she explained, "Since I came to America, I have been living in New Jersey. Like everybody, we have had some ups and downs. But I am so grateful I did not encounter any harm. The city of Jersey City, where I have been rooted, never failed me. I worked hard to take care of my family. My children went to school. We are all okay. Now I want to give something back to the community where I live. I am not an expert in anything. I know I cannot save the world. For my God, my community, and for my own peace of mind, I will not stay with my mouth shut.

"If I can tell a mother, 'Do not use foul language when your children are around,' if I can tell a father, 'Please do not drink and smoke in front of your kids,' and if at least one paid attention for even one minute, I'll be satisfied. My work is not vain. It is just a way to say thanks to God. It is also a way to say, 'Jersey, my love, thank you.'"

Before he left, Hyppolite went and knocked at Anne Marie's door. She was still upset, but she knew he was more flexible, easier going. She did not keep a long conversation, but she said enough about her problem.

"Little sister, my dear, you must learn to take care of yourself. Be patient and compassionate to yourself as you would with others. Believe you are worthy of great love the same as you believe another is worthy of yours. Too much stress is bad for both the mind and the body. If Mohammad is causing you to be in this state of stress, you need to look seriously at making significant changes. Consider this man like a dripping faucet that won't stop until you fix it. If the drip

got too irritating you can't stand it anymore, it is time to do something. Think about it. You're too young and too beautiful for all this."

Anne Marie spent the whole evening sitting in in her room
heavyhearted and undecided. By the time she went to the kitchen to
grab a bottle of water, the whole house was quiet. Méralie's door was
closed; her brothers and nephew were sleeping. The clock marked
exactly 1:00 a.m. She went back in her room and leaned on the
windowsill. In the silence of the night, the recollections of the past
invaded her mind, flashing back the good and not too good, censur-
ing her.

*How did we get to this? Was he joking when he promised to kill the
boy? Does anybody really know him? Why such a rush to leave Jersey City?*

As she started to get dizzy, it seemed that the shadow of
Mohammad was moving among the cars at the parking lot. Suddenly
she felt her feet losing ground, like she was in a big black hole, falling
in a precipice. Frightened and trembling, she slowly moved away
from the window and dropped herself on the bed, curling in a ball.

The next day, she opened her eyes with the morning sun hitting
her face through the window. When she realized she was still wearing
the clothes and shoes from yesterday, she mobilized her courage and
strength; and with a mechanical and resigned gesture, she picked up
the cellular, sending a message to Mohammad:

> I remember, when we first met, our hearts
> rejoiced; we sparkled with happiness. I thought
> it was forever. But soon I realized dreams are
> something that cannot always come true. Love
> is like a precious plant that needs to be nurtured
> with trust, understanding, affection, and respect.
> You are angry all the time. I do not have a space
> to breathe anymore, and the pressure is almost
> frightening.
>
> You need a girl that will stick by you no
> matter what you do. Unfortunately there is no
> future for us. I wish you the best, but you and I,
> we're done!

As Time Goes By

Happy days, moments sublime
When being at the right place at the right time
Like flowers opening to the morning light
Life is ahead, so sweet, so bright
The beginning of what seems to have no end
Is reaching out, extending an amicable hand
It is inviting; it's marvelous; it's tempting
How nice it is to be healthy and strong
What's more beautiful, breathe freely
Feel the joy of living; tread the ground boldly
The time for love, friendship, and adventure
Go without hesitation; still far is the future
The emotions are strong; happiness is near
The glory of youth is to celebrate with no fear
Spread the wings and soar; it is the moment
Run with the heart open to the present
But too soon, moves on the emblem of reality
Cascading over, displaying its print inexorably
The merrily years, as they go down day after day
Bumped across the time, tripped along the way
The gray ashes of the past cover the head
The frostbites of too many winters have spread
How? When? Who understands it?
Life is short; just seize the good of it
As the river doesn't go back to its source
Time takes the best in its course
Oh! The good old days of our lives
Treasured moments of our times
If the elders could and if the youths knew
Wasted opportunities are far and few

-21-

The Adolescents

Since Hyppolite last spoke with his sister, he tried to give her more attention. Although busy, he always found the time to pick her up when she needed, and he had been encouraging her to complete her exit papers. Raquel also had been supportive. One afternoon, they were all three sitting in the living room. Anne Marie told them she had been doing some research and wanted to elaborate on a project she would call "Another Opportunity." She dedicated this work to her nephew, Joseph, and her mother, who was so interested to see the youths straightened out.

All that time, Méralie was in the kitchen, putting pots and dishes in order. She overheard some words but did not pay much attention. As soon as they started speaking about the youths, she dropped everything to join the conversation.

"This is nice of you. For being a young person yourself, this is wise and courageous. I wished more and more people were interested in this noble cause. Youth, to me, means beauty, energy, innocence. It is defined as the appearance of freshness, vigor, and spirit. There is an intense desire to live and enjoy life in them. Back home where I was born, they give a lot of importance to the youths, for they are considered as the future of the family, the hope of the parents.

"After so many sacrifices—taking care of the kids, staying up at night, watching over them, investing every single penny in them— you are proud to say, 'This is my son or my daughter.' You keep them close to your heart, thanking God for every step they make and hoping, one day, they will take over but with better opportunity than you had in life.

"Life is so strange that you do not understand it," continued Méralie, nonstop. "Imagine a baby just born. You are looking at him, so small, so defenseless. You do not even notice when time had gone by. Before you blink an eye, he becomes taller than you. We all need to treat children with love and respect, love for the understanding and affection they need for the moment and respect for what they will become tomorrow. As the child is slowly leaving childhood, where the parents decide everything for him to enter adulthood, the time he will be on his own. He has important steps to take. These steps will define his future as an active and successful member of society."

"You are so right," cut Hyppolite in. "The choices they made are most likely to affect their future. I think their success depends in major part on their education and the environment they live in. A safe, healthy passage from adolescence into adulthood is the right of every child. To succeed in this, families and societies need to ensure that adolescents and youth acquire the knowledge and skills required to lead them to productive and fulfilling lives."

"In Jersey City," intervened Raquel, "the most protected investment is in the future, our children. The city is filled with elementary schools, colleges, and universities These academic institutions have given some of the most famous citizens acting now in the main political avenues of the country, making big decisions for generations of citizens to come."

"Unfortunately, some youths have encountered distractions that have lured them away from positive and more productive activities that would cultivate their leadership skills."

Anne Marie did not intervene. She was looking at everyone talking, but her mind seemed to be miles away. Since her last text message to Mohammad, she blocked his number, but still everything was too quiet, too dangerously calm. It was weird he did not give any sign of life. She could not find any explanation to it. This silence sounded like the calm before the storm.

"Are you with us, sister?" asked Hyppolite.

"Sorry," said Anne Marie, shaking her head. "I was thinking. The problem is not new. All over the world, there is a kind of revolution. Now, with the development of technology, everybody seems to be collected no matter how far they are. The drug and gang situation are a concerning problem to the world. Jersey City is not exempt, but they take it seriously. One case is too many, for the youth is the future of the community."

"What about the Another Opportunity Project?" asked Hyppolite.

"I am trying to promote a kind of motivation that will go hand in hand with this project. Opportunity is something you do not let slip through your hands, for it is a favorable occasion that doesn't come every day. But very often, people fail to make a difference simply because a golden opportunity has been offered to them too easy. Without goodwill and motivation, people cannot accomplish much."

"This is the truth," said Raquel. "My niece is now sixteen years old. She failed the class. The school gives a chance to review the material during summer vacation and go through another test to make up her grade. She did not study. She stayed behind. The problem is that she has been negligent with her work since the beginning of the scholar year. She did not care, so she lost the opportunity. Many people take for granted the help offered to them. Sometimes they start a project. They get a break for a while, and they fall back. Without self-conviction and determination, it is difficult to come through."

"Peer pressure is another cause of the problem," said Hyppolite. "Some youngsters are living in a situation where whatever they do is not good enough. If they got into fights, they are thugs. If they do not want to fight, they are punks. 'On both sides, the evil is endless.' Something must be done to conserve our values."

"It is said that pride can motivate people to strive for success," said Anne Marie. "They need something that can boost their emotion, motivation, and perception in a positive way."

"I remember Sister Laurieuse, a member of our church," said Méralie pensively. "She had so much trouble with her son, Leonard. When he was a kid, she used to help him every afternoon with his homework. As he got older and moved up to a higher grade, it became more difficult for the sister to follow the boy's work. When he was in the eleventh grade, he started to escape school. Every morning by eight o'clock, he would get dressed and leave the house, leading the mother to think that he was attending school. When he was sure the mother was at work, he would come back to the house by 9:00 a.m., sometimes with friends, to play his video games or sleep. He did not want to go to school or study a trade or anything. The sister got sick and tired of struggling with this boy. One year after, before the summer, he was asked to accompany a twelfth-grade girl to her prom. The day of the party, that boy was so elegantly dressed that, if there was any contest for best looking, he would win without any doubt.

"But something happened that made him change completely. He was sitting at a table with a group of friends, having a good time, when he saw an old girlfriend, his high school sweetheart. He immediately left the table to approach the girl, who happened to be in love with him. They spoke for a couple of minutes, touching base on what was going on with their lives, their studies, etc. The girl downright refused to see him again simply because he was not in school. He was not doing anything. 'I don't want to date a failure,' she said to him. The boy went home and isolated himself in his room for a whole week. No one knew what was on his mind. The next time he came outside was to direct himself straight back to Snyder High School and get reinstated in school for the next school year. He went back, never missed a day, and he completed high school being the head of the class. He did not stop there. He got enlisted in the navy, continued studying, and got married to that girl. That boy is now an honorable citizen, a professional, a good father, and a good husband. From a careless boy with no incentive, he become a respectable citizen, an active member of society."

"You have all said enough!" yelled Anne Marie with excitement. "Thank you. I have taken notes of all this information. My plan is to speak about a program that would be tailored specially for any teenager who already have problem with the law.

"He would have to work very hard, putting his thoughts together, acting as his own lawyer. The judge knows that he does not have the rhetoric of an advanced intellect who knows all the details of the legal field. But using his own words, taking responsibility, he would defend himself with the purpose to straighten out in life. He knows his neighborhood. He knows his weakness and limitations, and he also knows what it would take to help him away from the same mess.

"The compilation of all this indiscreet information will help the competent authorities to discern the problem and find a better way to help the young first offenders to stay clean."

"Anything that can contribute to help a young person is good," said Méralie. "Youth is not a period of timelessness when the horizons of age seem too far distant to be noticed. Whether they like it or not, the clock is ticking. Time is passing by. No one is young forever. If they insist on staying in their comfort zone—doing nothing positive, sleeping all day long, hanging out at night—they will be soon left behind. The time to prepare their life for the future is now, for they are the future of the community."

-22-

The Less Young Also Have Their Spot under the Sun

Hyppolite paid off the loan on the van earlier than predicted. He received different offers from car dealers and had the opportunity to buy two more vans. Although his brothers were pushing him to go for a package deal, he got one vehicle. Going too fast without a solid base, he thought, was not a good idea. He judged that the down payment he had been saving was not enough; better safe than sorry.

As usual, he was at his mother's house over the weekend, talking to his brothers, who were excited about the other acquisition. Hellen was sitting with Anne Marie, but from time to time, she would get up to use the bathroom. From the kitchen, Méralie was preparing dinner and enjoying the music coming from the living room. She approached Hellen to chat for a second.

"You look more beautiful every day. You are radiant," she said, holding Hellen's hand, looking at her nails. "How are you doing?"

"Okay. I am doing well."

Méralie was a very perceptive woman. She had been observing Hellen, who became so round, her skin and eyes so bright; she was suspicious but did not ask any indiscreet questions. By ten o'clock, the couple went home.

Méralie called Anne Marie in her room and asked, "What's up with Hellen? Is she all right?"

"She is all right, I think. Nobody mentioned anything."

The following Wednesday, Hyppolite was in the neighborhood; he stopped by the house to check on his mother, who started asking questions.

"How is your life with Hellen? Do you both have any problems?"

"Hellen is very understanding, nice, and loving. I am so grateful that I met her. I followed a lot of her advice to get to this point in the business."

"Did you leave a woman in Haiti?"

"No! Why?"

"If not, why you two refusing to get married? Why didn't you tell me Hellen is expecting a baby?"

"It was Tertulien, right?" said Hyppolite, surprised. "That tattletale of a brother. He is the one who told you. He couldn't keep his mouth shut just for a couple of weeks. He had to gossip."

"Nobody told me anything, but I am not stupid. I just look at Hellen. I was talking to her in the living room, and as soon as I looked at her fingernails that happened not to be polished, I noticed she was pregnant. Now, if everybody knew, I would like to know why you hid it from me."

"It's not that," responded Hyppolite, embarrassed.

"When I married your father, I was twenty-five years old," continued Méralie, who started a new sermon. "We have created a family, a lifelong commitment. Things were not too easy, but we had lived with integrity, respect, and dignity. We had a stable home. You and Hellen, you are two responsible adults who decided to live together. If you love each other, you should seal this relationship in a solid foundation. Where there is love, the bond between a man and a woman can last all the days of their lives. Marriage provides the grace to grow into a union of the heart and soul. It also provides stability for the couple and the children to come. People respect that. God planned for men and women to unite in love for the continuity of his creation, the human family. A child is a gift of life, a blessing from God. The family provides a framework for each of its members to develop as a person in love and security. Please think about it. If a baby is coming, he needs a mother, a father, and a secure home."

Méralie spoke to her son for a long time. Since she was already dressed, Hyppolite, on his way back, took her to Journal Square.

Wednesday in summer is a special day for Jersey City. It is the farmers market day, a day that brings neighbors and friends together. Acting under the Department of Agriculture, the farmers market is one of the most highly anticipated events of spring and summer in Jersey City. It always brings an exciting and creative addition to Journal Square shopping center, enhancing the area with activity and energy. Since early morning, tents and tables are set up, ready to receive "New Jersey's bounty," the freshest, healthiest locally grown produce brought directly from the farm. Lying at the side of the Bergen Avenue, monopolizing McGinley Square, the farmers market offers all kind of goods; but the mouthwatering fruits and vegetables are proudly displayed all over the farmers' tables. As you look at the golden tomatoes and the gorgeous eggplants and green pepper, they sparkle like black diamonds at the jewelry store. Much more, musical entertainment is always there to reinforce the fun. Every week, a different group brings a different beat from a different culture to the public. From rock and roll to salsa and merengue, the fun is always complete. The air is filled with sweet and warm musical notes, pushing people passing by to shake their body even if for a second.

Around noon, the market is at its peak. People who are working in banks and offices nearby and students from the schools in the area swarm the square like bees, taking advantage of their lunchtime to make their provisions of fruits for the week. It is always crowded, blooming with beautiful young people full of energy, all races and all colors shopping and having a good time.

But the fun is not only for the active population. In Jersey City, the less young, the senior citizens, also have their spot under the sun. The farmers market is one of their favorite places. They would sit on the cement benches, talking to each other and enjoying the fresh breeze cooling down the weather.

Weirdly enough, this was the only place besides church Méralie would hang out weekly with some elderly sisters. Before doing their shopping, they would take their time to talk about their grandchildren, reminisce over past time and, most of all, exchange news from

Haiti, the beloved and faraway land that they would like to see one more time before they closed their eyes.

Filled with energy, people were eating, dancing, enjoying the wholesome experiences of talking to farmers about produce, and seeing their neighbors or friends out in the open air; Bergen Avenue, Kennedy Boulevard, and the streets surrounding the square were in full swing. Inside the square itself, the activities were not less; boutiques, restaurants, and other businesses opened on the lower level could not complain about lack of customers.

The subways were working on normal schedule. The Path train coming from Penn Station in Newark made its regular stop at Journal Square to let people on and off. The passengers, always too busy to pay attention to other people or to even say hello, quickly made their move and disappeared.

"Attention, attention, closing doors. Next stop, Grove Street," announced the loudspeaker before the train continued its trajectory.

"This is my stop!" yelled Albert, who nodded off on the ride.

He jumped his seat, grabbed his bag, and rushed out of the door that was closing on him. Feeling a bit dizzy, he sat on the bench for a while, looking at the train moving away. In a long and indiscreet yawn, he stretched his arm and legs, fixed his cap over his head, and walked his way up to the streets.

On the sidewalk, Albert looked around and felt strange. He had not seen the square for a long time. He did not remember Wednesdays in the summer being so active or people enjoying it so much.

The point is things have changed a great deal. Community farmers markets in New Jersey are more popular today than ever because exceeding numbers of consumers have more awareness of health and nutrition. They are becoming interested in buying their fresh produce directly from local farmers.

Albert was looking at the people walking around, eating, and conversing; some were dancing to the sound of the popular merengue rhythm.

The singer, a young Dominican man, kept everyone tied up with his charming voice, "Juliana que mala eres, que mala eres Juliana."

The square's clock marked exactly 2:45 p.m. Albert had not eaten since morning. He crossed the street, entered the McDonald's, and ordered a cheeseburger before going to the bus station. At first glance, he thought nothing had changed commute wise. The Kennedy Boulevard, Bergen Avenue, and West Side Avenue buses were running on schedule as usual. But it was only inside the bus he noticed that the fare was no longer $1.00; he needed $1.50 to ride home. He got off the bus and took to the road on foot.

Méralie was sitting with some sisters when two neighbors passing by stopped to greet them. She invited them to sit with her, and the conversation switched to the youths in the neighborhood. After only two minutes of convincing them, one of the ladies, a middle-aged woman, gripped her hands. At that moment, it was like a bond; an affinity started to build between them. She stared at her with a look of anxiety across her face.

"I do not know how much I can do at this stage of my life," she said. "My legs sometimes do not respond. I feel like time is running out on me. The sun is setting, but it never too late to do a good deed. I completely understand what you are talking about. God gave us children, and he also gives us a heart to love them. Since the moment they were born, they are the center of our lives. Our helplessness increases. We try to raise them, mold, and shape them after our best knowledge and endeavor. Very often, we come up short. We realize that they have their own personality. But that does not mean we have to throw our hands in the air and give up.

"My daughter has three beautiful children. She was okay, taking care of them, raising them. Suddenly—I do not know what happened—she got involved with illicit business, and she ran away with a man. Last thing I heard from her, she was doing time in jail, and her children are now my responsibility."

"I am thinking about life nowadays," said Méralie with sadness, "and I wonder where the good old times have gone. I remember back home, I was young. There weren't any drugs, gangs, or weapons going around. At least I didn't see or heard anything like that. But whenever anybody stood in the middle of the yard or the front porch and yelled crick, others would respond crack. Kids and young adults would come running, ready to sit down and listen the most beautiful stories from our oral traditions. You say pot, the beans were getting ready to be cooked. You said marijuana, people would think that you are talking about the lady up the block. You said dust, you are thinking about cleaning. At that time, people did not have so much luxury or technology, but it was less complicated. Kids were growing up safer, and parents were more at peace. Things have changed. Now these innocent words sound like big trouble."

"Now there is no respect," said another lady. "People are going around swearing, lying. A constant stream of gutter filth laced with obscenities is coming from the mouths of men and women. You turn on the TV, the hells, the damns, and all sorts of vulgarities spew out of it. There is no consideration for kids or the elderly, not even for God."

"But we have a moral responsibility toward our family and our community," cut Méralie in a more serious tone. "If only we can tell a young mother, 'Make sure the kids do their homework and go to bed on time.' If a mother can only censure what the kids are watching on television, that would be great. We cannot do much, but we can express ourselves. We can give advice, some words of wisdom, speak about God. What about we start talking to our own family, children, grandchildren, and relatives? Just subtlety with respect, understanding, and lot of patience, we'll get some to listen."

Méralie was in the middle of the conversation when someone touched her shoulder. She turned her head; a young man was standing there, smiling at her. She pulled a paper towel from her pocket, cleaned her glasses, and readjusted them to her face.

"Albert!" she said. "When did you come home?"

"I just got released today. I am on my way home."

Méralie excused herself from her friends and left with Albert helping her carrying the groceries she just purchased. Without any doubt, she would not miss the opportunity to lecture him and preach him the Gospel of the Lord.

Anne Marie's thesis was a success. She was coming out of the college with Raquel, happy for completing her studies in criminal justice. The day was nice, so instead of going home, they walked around the square window-shopping. From there, they continued along Kennedy Boulevard, enjoying the sunshine and the fresh breeze. Eventually they stopped at a restaurant and ate something. As they were walking, they were talking and laughing. Anne Marie seemed to be relaxed and happy. At the corner of Kennedy Boulevard and Newark Avenue, a boy approached her and handed her a note. Instantly her heart jumped, and her mind went to Mohammad. Shaking a bit, she anxiously opened the piece of paper and read:

> Your words hit like bullets.
> My heart is badly shattered,
> That the pieces no longer fit together.
> Now I looked at myself in the mirror.
> I do not recognize the face staring back at me.
> Congratulations on the mess you made of me.
> You are going to regret losing me.
> When you realize it and try to come back,
> Just know it will be too late.

Visibly uncomfortable, Anne Marie's face reddened like a tomato. She turned around and walked back. Raquel did not want her to be alone in the streets; she followed her.

From the square, they walked straight down Bergen Avenue and went past Highland Avenue, Glenwood, Mercer Street. Meanwhile, police cars and ambulance were going by with their loud and pro-longed sirens. At the corner of Bergen and Fairmont avenues, the traffic was diverted to another direction, and a crowd gathered there watching like something big was going on. During all that noise and commotion, Anne Marie did not look right or left.

Like on automatic, she continued at the same rapid pace, wiggling through the crowd until someone yelled out loud, "Anne Marie!"

She suddenly stopped, looked down, and could not believe her eyes. Tossed on the ground in the middle of the street were three men facedown, handcuffed like common criminals; Mohammad was one of them.

"Mohammad!" she said, shaking like a leaf.

Raquel instantly grabbed her, pushed her to the side, and hugged her. She became hysterical, crying and yelling. Raquel could not wait for the Uber she called. In that moment, a number 87 bus was going by. They jumped in and sat behind the driver.

Another passenger who got on the bus after them told the whole story, "All three who got arrested are drug lords. One of them, Mohammad, was away for a while. This dude is crazy. He is a street hustler well-known in every drug area where there is chaos. He is very smart. His business name is Kiki. He has a habit of manipulating single females who seem to be good girls when he is really a coldhearted man. He has no remorse or feelings for anybody. I do not know what happened. He was standing at the corner with another dude name Louissaint when the fight broke with some men driving by. It seems that a deal went sour. They started shooting, and then Louissaint got hit. The ambulance took him to the hospital."

When they got to the building where she lived, Anne Marie opened the door with demeanor that begged explanation. As soon as Méralie saw her, she felt something was terribly wrong.

"What happened?" she asked

Anne Marie starred down at her feet, ashamed, and took refuge in her room. Raquel had no choice but to tell what was going on. When Méralie remembered that Louissaint was the young man she met not too long ago coming from the liquor store, an intense sadness and a feeling of emptiness and hopelessness invaded her.

"So many people died at a tender age because of violence. They did not have time to enjoy life, to live as a decent human being. Life is like a bubble in the stream, a spark that flies upward from an autumnal bonfire. It flames for a moment against the night sky and is then extinguished forever. So short a distance between our hellos and our goodbyes. Life is too short. Time is too precious, and the stakes are too high to be living astray, going crazy, and be playing around."

Part 5
Together Forever

No matter how hard you get beat up,
No matter how tough the suffering is,
There is always a seed of love left:
Look deep inside!

-23-

Breaking News

We are already in September. The summer heat, gradually cooling down, gives way too much pleasant weather, leading rapidly toward the cold. People put aside sleeveless dresses, shorts, and sandals; but the outdoor fun continues. Every season has its spirit, a character of its own, and fall is particularly enchanted and famous for its harvest abundance. It seems nature has turned inside out to render all of earth's wonders, pushing farmers and consumers to look forward for a big Thanksgiving celebration.

In the Garden State, fruits and vegetables flourish; and back-to-school time, as always, is right on schedule for the harvest fun. From apple picking to hayrides and corn mazes, teachers and students enjoy visiting the farms. These seasonal festivities last until November, and the New Jersey farmers keep their doors open for family fun activities.

The breakup of Anne Marie and Mohammad was hurtful. In the beginning, she was so stubborn she did not want to hear any advice and was ready to shut anybody up. Now she realized it was not a good idea to be too arrogant. The last incident involving his public arrest was even more painful. Her pride was hurt. She felt debased, humiliated, and so ashamed that she did not want to face anyone. The overwhelming frustration of the past three months had debilitated and weighed her down to her knees. It was so stressful no one could help ease the agony she had been carrying. On the verge of an emotional meltdown, she was surrounded by darkness. She spent almost two weeks disconnected to the world. Her television and phone were off. She just went to work and came back home. Her room had become her sanctuary. The family was worried; and on different occasions, the boys spoke to Méralie, calling for a meeting.

"Anne Marie has changed. She does not talk much. She eats in her room. It seems she is avoiding us. We understand she feels embarrassed, but if she continues like this, she will fall into depression. I think the whole family should band together to encourage and help her get out of this worrisome mood."

"Leave her alone for a while," said Méralie in a disciplinary tone. "You all know how much I love my daughter, but time-out is not only for children. Adults need it too. Give her space to think, to meditate and figure out her life from this point on. To grow in age, wisdom, and grace, to be more effective and sustainably successful, we have got to knock out the arrogance, the know-it-all. Sometimes embarrassment, humiliation are good tools. They are necessary to keep us humble and spiritually clean. It is tough, but you need to separate the poison of the ego from the real self. This will free our soul and make us more effective to fulfillment. Anne Marie is strong enough to withstand this. We are not going to bring her a box of tissues on a golden tray to dry her eyes. She needs to pick up her strength, splash water on her face, catch her reflection in the mirror, and decide how to behave."

It is now official; fall is in the air. Mother Nature is changing right before our eyes. The bright green summer leaves are turning yellow, orange, and brown, adding an incredibly special accent to the beginning of the season. The weather is perfect, and the holiday spirit is on the rise. It is a beautiful time of year, but it goes fast. In Hudson County, the residents take no time to start their decorations; and if you are a good observer, you will swear that autumn is their favorite. From Bayonne to North Bergen, every front door is decorated with the most beautiful accents of autumn. Hanging baskets of harvest foliage and berries are placed everywhere. Pumpkins of all sizes and all shapes replace the summer flower pots in front of gates and porches. Who does not love pumpkin carving? It is messy, but it fun. It is the time people put their creativity to the test.

In the building where the family lived, a huge pumpkin was placed in the vestibule with a dry bouquet with vivid colors to create a warm welcome. The aromatic smell of cinnamon and honeysweet essence touched your senses as soon as you open the security door; the maintenance crew had done a really good job.

Encouraged by the display, Esaie and Tertulien wanted to bring the spirit of fall into the apartment. They went to the farm on Route 440 and brought two nice-size pumpkins and some flowers. They placed them in the kitchen and the living room, hoping they would cheer up their sister; Méralie was pleased. Hellen was an expert in home decoration; the next time she came over, she would add her special touch. Hyppolite already called for everybody to be in the house; he had another announcement. This time, dinner was on him.

Méralie, since the last meeting with the boys, thought that Anne Marie had to learn from her own mistakes. If she chose the solitude of her room, so be it. However, her mother's heart did not resist. Knowing that she was in pain, she tried several times to speak to her, at least to know what she thought; but she changed her mind. Finally she took courage and went knocking on her door.

"How are you?" she said, wanting to have a conversation. "Your nephew wants you to accompany him to the farm this Saturday. What do you think?"

"My head hurts," said Anne Marie. "I am sorry I can't accompany Joseph."

"You cannot remain in the dark. Autumn has always been your favorite season. At least open your curtains. Let some fresh air pass through."

"Don't open the window," cried Anne Marie.

Méralie was looking at her daughter's face against the wall like a kid being punished. She stood in the room for a while, willing to accompany her in her pain.

"Autumn has something mysterious from which we can learn a lesson of wisdom," she said with a lower tone of voice. "There is a time for everything in life, a time for joy, a time for sadness, a time to sow, and a time to harvest. Spring grows leaves and flowers. Fall sheds the leaves. The same way, we should know there is a time we accumulate frustration and pain. We go through trials and tribulations, but there is also a time to release things that have been a burden. Think about it. I am leaving the window open. You will close it if you want."

At about five o'clock in the afternoon, a cold air gradually invaded the room. Anne Marie got up to draw the curtains. From the window, she looked at the trees around the parking lot. Slowly and gradually, they are already beginning to lose their glorious green glow. One by one, the leaves, carried away by the breeze, floated on the ground.

Very soon, they will be completely stripped, she thought. *The bare branches will go through the freezing cold of winter, but there is still hope for a new spring. The future will bring new energy, new life, and again they will be covered with green leaves full of sap.*

Anne Marie remained at her bedroom window for a long time. In the silence of her room, she would like to have the wisdom of nature and renew her life like trees after winter, but the more she thought, the more she felt bad.

The problem was not Mohammad. He was no longer in the picture since she took the decision to text him out of her life. The real issue was the baggage of the negative feelings that were weighing her down—the shame and the remorse for being too naive. People in the neighborhood knew who the man was. So many times, she walked down the streets of Jersey City happily holding his hand. How could she make such a fool of herself? She did not have the nerve enough to go back out there and face the public.

She then remembered the last sermon of her mother: "If you fall, don't stay on the ground, having pity on yourself, waiting for people to come and cry with you. Just get up, shake the dirt off, and continue your way. Give thanks that you don't have any broken bones. Learn from your mistakes, but don't dwell on them."

Anne Marie realized that she could not control people's thinking or the situation around her. But she did not have to surrender her dreams, her joy, and her life. She went into the shower and let the water fall on her for a long time as if she wanted to wash not only her body but also her mind.

No more crying. No more negative thinking, she told herself.

All that time she was struggling with her own emotions and Mohammad's pressure and insistence, she did not give up work. She

continued her school until completion. She realized she was stronger than she thought. Her faith was hurt, but she did not have to lose hope. She needed to gather the strength she had left to crawl her way out of that deep hole of bitterness. She realized God had been with her the whole time.

On Saturday morning, she woke up bright and early and turned the light and the music on. For more than two weeks, the light, the radio, and her cell phone were completely off. She was sitting in the dark and in silence as if she were punishing herself. As she started to clean her room, she gathered letters, pictures, and any piece of paper that had to do with Mohammad. And while sweeping under the dresser, she found a single birthday card that was not from him.

My dear Annie,

I would like to strip the gardens in Jersey City of their most beautiful roses. I would like to steal the sweetest notes from the most romantic music and collect the brightest stars from the Haitian sky that never knew the winter season to make a special bouquet today, the day of your birth. Since time and distance are failing me, please accept these roses with my heart that is beating only for you.

Benoit

Anne Marie stopped for a minute. This boy had been in love with her since junior high school. Mohammad was aggressive, insistent, and more manipulative with his words. He swept her off her feet, but the way he dealt with women did not sit well with her. Anne Marie read the birthday card and, with a quick gesture, threw it in the garbage can along with the other notes. All these memories, good or bad, she wanted to pile them up together with the autumn leaves and make a bonfire out of them.

She then went to the kitchen to prepare breakfast. To the surprise of the family, she was smiling again. The cell phone that used to be glued on her ear or on her hands as she texted out of control was sitting on the counter. Anne Marie looked relaxed and well centered.

Méralie gathered her strength and took a deep breath; and once again, she shouted, "Alleluia! Praise the Lord!"

By Sunday afternoon, Hyppolite and Hellen were headed to the house. From the front of the building, a rich flavor of something cooking invaded the neighborhood. People passing by would be turning their head, trying to find out who was cooking. The couple went up the stairs, only to find out that the cooking flavor was coming from the kitchen. Anne Marie was setting the table and had everything ready for dinner. Hyppolite was happy to see her in a more relaxed mood. Since everybody was there, he invited the ladies to sit down; and in an impressive and inspiring way, he did not take any time to make the big announcement.

"You have been at my side in the most difficult moments of my life. I am grateful for your patience. Hellen and I, we love each other. But thanks to my mother who didn't stop talking faith in us, we realize that a child is a gift of life, a blessing. We need to be ready to receive him in a family. Today we want to bring you the good news. We are planning to get married by the end of December."

Anne Marie was touched. She felt that part of this speech was a godsent message to her.

Méralie was moved to tears. "Marriage is the foundational relationship for all of society. It is an institution created by God and, therefore, is holy and sacred.

"I pray that God blesses this union and the children to come. I am not asking for riches, but I would like to see all my children in a family united with love and peace. Since everybody is here together, I would like to say something very touching and dear to me. And even when I am no longer on this earth, I want you to remember this. It is about an American tradition. To me, it is one of the best. I do not know why family reunions are so thoughtful, so beautiful!

"I was the first from my family to come to America. At that time, Jersey City did not have many Haitian people, and I did not know English. Communication was a big problem. I was lonely. I was dying of nostalgia.

"In the neighborhood, I used to see these kinds of gatherings every year. People would come from all over to get together in one group. But it took me time to understand the importance of these meetings. Where I come from, we did not have this beautiful tradition. Because the family and the extended family were mostly close by, everybody is confined in one area. The grandfather, for example, had children. The children had children and so forth. They built their house on the same premises or habitation. But America is a well-developed country. The families are emancipated. The children went far to study, and they did not come back. They established themselves all over. That makes sense for everybody to gather at least once a year and touch base, to meet the new members and refresh memories. I think you should adopt this good tradition and encourage your children to continue generation after generation.

"And secondly please teach your children to speak Creole, your native language. It is always good to know more than one language."

Once the meeting was over, everybody gathered around the table, eating, talking to each other, and celebrating the good news. Hellen brought lots of food, but Méralie's soup was a phenomenon. Hellen asked for the recipe. Raquel, who was invited, asked for the recipe.

"I did not cook a regular meal," said Méralie, "but since it started to be cold, I knew you would like it."

"You make this soup every year," said Esaie. "I want the recipe too for Yanique. We are planning our wedding, but it is not official yet."

"This soup is called soup joumou," continued Méralie. "It is a tradition in the Haitian culture. On January 1, we celebrate the new year and Haiti's independence. It was on that date Haiti became the first country to have ever successfully revolted against slavery. So as Haitians, we take great pride in our history. We celebrate each year with this traditional soup. It is a warm, hearty, and deliciously made of pureed squash, combined with spices, vegetables, beef, and pasta. In every spoon, it carries a special meaning, one that represents hope and freedom! More than just a regular soup, the soup joumou is history that should never be forgotten."

At the end, Hellen served a cake made with product freshly harvested, a delicacy of the season. Now she was ready to see the fall decoration material the boys brought. Her magic touch would surely bring a charm to the apartment. Esaie and Tertulien looked for the pumpkins all over the house. They went to their mother, asking where she put them; Hellen was waiting.

"What pumpkin?" said Méralie with a funny smile across her face.

The boys looked at each other and then turned their gaze to Anne Marie.

"I do not have anything to do with that," she said before disappearing to her room.

Everybody finally realized that the delicious and finger-licking soup they just ate was made from the pumpkins; Méralie had cooked both. It was a nice evening full of surprises: Anne Marie had returned to herself and her good mood. The official announcement of Hellen and Hyppolite's wedding had brought lots of joy. Even the soup brought new awareness. They used pumpkin all the time, but they did not know it could make such delicious soup.

Before she left, Raquel spoke to Anne Marie.

"I am glad to see you smiling. The last time I brought you home, you were a complete mess. I called many times. You did not answer or return my calls. I was worried, but I did not want to drop in just like that. I want to tell you do not be too hard on yourself. Do not punish yourself too much. We all have bias based on whatever our own story and life experience has been. But we need to let the past be the past and move forward. Your only crime was to trust a man who does not deserve your love. I do not even want to mention his name. He is away for a long time. He will not be around to make your life impossible. Do not dwell on what happened, on things you cannot change."

"Do not worry. I am okay. During the past three months, I have been through hell and back. I have struggled with ridding myself of guilt, shame, and grief. I have struggled freeing myself from mistakes, a bad relationship, and worries. Now I am better. I have my mind made up."

"God will breathe on your effort, and he will give strength and ability to hold on."

-24-

A Moment of Peace

The fall season in the Garden State is fabulous. From Passaic, Hudson, Essex, and Union counties, the big tourist attractions during spring and summer have momentously put on an outfit that would marvel you from afar or near. It seems that, high above, a solid golden wall has exploded in sparks and the sky opens its windows and blows an autumnal wave over the trees and bushes, magically touching the leaves.

It is such a beautiful time of year, the time everything bursts with its last beauty, as if nature had been saving up all year for the grand finale. In the morning, when the sun breaks over, touching the giant trees, bringing a new shine to the vibrant color of the leaves, the spectacle is breathtaking. No other place and no other leaves seem as golden as the ones in the Garden State.

It takes a summer and a winter to have autumn. These two are so aggressive. They squeezed it so tight and so thin in the middle that it shies away fast. Before you know it, the last leaf is trembling on the branches, and the birds have flown to their wintering ground. That is one the reasons Raquel was pushing, encouraging Anne Marie to get back on her feet, to go for it before she missed all the fun.

Benoit had also been trying to get closer to the family. As a young Haitian American man, he was able to identify himself with the boys, talking about sports, music, and politics. On different occasions, they watched the soccer game together from the CONCACAF Championship. He was still in love with Anne Marie, but she seemed uninterested. Nevertheless, he did not lose hope. He was not pushy like Mohammad, but patience and perseverance were his strength.

Anne Marie spoke to Hyppolite about him. She expressed fear because of her recent experience.

"Since the beginning, the whole family did not have a good impression about Mohammad," said Hyppolite. "I am not here to judge you. People sometimes are misled by their own heart. They fight for something that was doomed to fail from the start. I guess, because you loved him, you trusted him. You cared, but you could not change him. Do not punish yourself for that. Your value does not decrease based on someone else's inability to see your worth. You were strong enough to walk back from that dead end.

"When we face difficult situations and get a solution out of it, we empower our self. We become smarter, stronger than before. I trust you on this. Someday everything will make perfect sense. For the moment, do not dwell too much on this. Believe in yourself, smile, go on with your life, and remember, everything happens for a reason."

On Saturday, Raquel picked up Anne Marie and her nephew, Joseph, for a tour around some farms close by; they were supposed to meet up with Benoit and his young brother, Harold. All along the way, the tree-lined roads offered the same golden spectacle nuanced with reddish and brown colors. They finally got to the most precious farm at Monmouth County, where they had a good time. Joseph and Harold were becoming restless, playing and kicking the leaves on the ground. A couple of times, Anne Marie went quiet for a while; no one knew what was on her mind. Benoit tried to cheer her up without asking any question.

"I can feel you are not joyful like before. The heart has treasures well kept, the thoughts, the hopes, the dreams, the aspirations, but it also hides painful memories. No one, not even poets, has ever measured how much a heart can hold. Sometimes it is so sealed maybe it will never be revealed. I have known you since we were teenagers. I pray you regain confidence and your joy. You are a fountain of goodness and gladness. Around you, people breathe peace and feel like smiling. This is a blessing. It is good to take a day at a time. Do not look forward to an uncertain future or backward to the past.

"Live the moment. Look around you. Nowhere is more beautiful than this spectacle nature is offering right now. Smile. Breathe the fresh air. Smell the rich flavor of the ripened fruits. This is marvelous. Let us take some pictures and capture this beautiful panorama before it is gone."

Joseph and Harold ran up to Anne Marie's side, posing for the picture, yelling, "Cheese!"

Anne Marie spontaneously wrapped her arms around their shoulders, repeating, "Cheese!" a smile that would be kept forever in a memorable autumnal landscape.

As the week rolled around, people at Méralie's house had no other conversation but the wedding of Hyppolite and Hellen. The anxiety and the rush for things to be meticulously correct gave the impression they would not be able to execute the whole plan on time. It was Sunday evening; as usual, everybody was together. Anne Marie was in the room with Hellen and Yanique, putting the last points in place: the different color dresses, the design for the flower girls, the maid of honor, etc.

"Men are less complicated," said Hellen, looking at Hyppolite and his brothers sitting in the living room watching TV. "They just need their tuxedo, a nice haircut, and they are ready."

In fact, the brothers were watching a soccer game. According to them, it was a particularly important match: Mexico versus Brazil. Lost, body and soul in the game, they were yelling, throwing their feet and arms like they were the players at the stadium. Every goal was a commotion, an interminable cry of joy. Suddenly everything stopped, not for commercial, but for breaking news.

"We interrupt our regular programming for a special bulletin. Gruesome discovery in a garage in Jersey City! A woman was found bleeding on the highway. She was taken to the hospital, where she spent three months in a coma. Police finally got a break on the case. They went to a garage with a warrant to question a person of interest. There, they discovered human body parts wrapped in a plastic bag inside a freezer. Two arrests have been made. As the investigation continues, we will keep you informed."

At that moment, Joseph happened to be passing by the living room.

"Papa, look!" he said, pointing at the TV.

From the images broadcasted, one of the men arrested was Takeema's boyfriend, who was still living across the street.

The news sent shivers down the spines of the three men. Sitting there staring at the TV like living dead, they were trembling in cold sweat. The game came back on; no one paid attention. Esaie's heart was racing to his throat. He took a deep breath and sought to rationalize a moment, trying to make a sense to the news. After so long, why now? How?

Just for curiosity, Hellen was going to the living room to ask what happened to the game. Why did they become so silent? Who won? When they saw her coming, Esaie and Tertulien grabbed Hyppolite by the arms and rushed out to the parking lot.

"I have been telling you," said Hyppolite, trembling. "I had the premonition that package was going to resurface. It is coming back to haunt us."

"This bad habit of losing control when something happens," said Esaie, "you need to quit that! It's true that life is not always fair. A lot of innocent people are victims without any reason. But you are a man. You need to be strong. If you know deep down that you did not do anything wrong, do not carry yourself like you are losing it. You are not a suspect. Hold your head high. Square your shoulders. Look up. Remember mother's word, 'You are the son of the highest God.' I refuse to panic, losing my mind like the last time. I have an unshakable faith that we will get out of this trap."

While following them to the van, Hellen overheard Esaie. She was looking at them with a puzzled look across the face, surprise evident in her eyes.

"What trap are you in? What is going on?"

Not knowing that Hellen was following them, the men did not know where to start. Esaie took a deep breath, looked over at Hyppolite, and tilted his head as a sign to go ahead and speak. But Hyppolite, a man who used to speak so freely, using his language skill so effectively to charm an audience, was mute this time. Even Esaie, who had such a persuasive speech, was staring at Hellen without a word.

"To hell with all of this!" burst out Tertulien, finally. "We did not do anything wrong. We know it. God knows it. When Hyppolite came to live with us, he was traumatized by the earthquake. He was lucky to be alive. As a responsible man, he immediately applied for jobs. While waiting, he turned to the transportation business. Shortly after, something very disturbing happened. Some passengers left a package with damning evidence of a crime inside the van. As you understand, we were all shocked, thinking what we should do. The worst part of it, the package disappeared without a trace before we had time to say or do anything.

"Since then, we have not had peace. We have been living in confusion, uncertainty. We never stopped thinking of what would happen if that thing resurfaced one day. Now we just heard it on the news. Police found the package in possession of a man across the street. I feel we are in a bad predicament. It is like having a Damocles sword hanging over our head."

"I do not understand all these trials and tribulations," lamented Esaie. "Why? Is it karma, destiny, or bad luck? When you respect yourself, when you are working hard to make a living, drama comes directly to you to destroy your life."

"Stop!" said Hellen, visibly nervous. "I want to hear from Hyppolite himself. When did this happen? Why didn't you go to the police? Why didn't you tell me anything? Please do not hide anything from me."

Hyppolite picked up his strength and tried to give the best explanation possible. Hellen remembered that Friday evening when the standstill traffic got everybody nervous at the Holland Tunnel. Police with dogs were checking, looking for an escapee. She also remembered when those men got in the van with a container and took off running, leaving the door open.

"This is very delicate," said Hellen. "You need to do something before the investigations point out to you. At the law firm where I work, they conduct criminal investigations for court appearance. Let me speak to one of the lawyers. As a matter of fact, I think I have something that can help. One of the men had a tattoo on his left arm that looked like a zodiac sign. I took a picture of it when he was moving around. I have his arm and the right side of the other man's face."

Two weeks after, Hellen called them with good news. The police got a break on the case. The three brothers finally let out the breath they had been holding for so long.

Based on forensic evidence, the victim was identified. The investigations led to the perpetrators, who confessed to the crime. The man across the street could not explain how the package got to his freezer. He had no relationship with the perpetrators, but he was still in prison for domestic violence. As for Takeema, the medical diagnoses revealed that she suffered from aphasia. The man's ill treatment caused her a stroke of the brain, resulting in the loss of speech. Her relatives took her to North Carolina.

"I do not know what explanation I am going to give my mother and my sister," said Hyppolite. "Sooner or later, they will have to know."

"I do not think it is a good idea," said Esaie. "Let us pray that the problem is solved once and for all. Our mother is old. I noticed how these kinds of things affect her.

"Anne Marie is still delicate after her breakup with Mohammad. She was aware of a problem we had, but she never knew what it was exactly. I think we should leave these two alone."

Méralie had not spoken to anyone about her letter to *Jersey Journal*. Hyppolite, who had accompanied her that day, was on his guard, checking the newspaper daily. The following Tuesday, while on the streets, he stopped at a magazine stand and got the *Journal*. As he began turning the pages, he stopped on a poem that touched his heart. Standing there thinking and thinking, he shook his head; the words of this open letter seemed very familiar to him:

Dear Jersey,

The children have become restless.
Running with frustration and *bitterness*,
They are in search of fathers,

That, for some, nothing matters.
Mom's attention, precious treasure,
Leading hand to a better future,
For giving up too soon, is neither here.
Jersey, you are out there.
Do not give up on them; I know you do care.
Raise the lantern a bit higher.
Show them the way; pull them closer.
Help them grow better and wiser.
These youngsters are your sons and daughters.
The Garden needs these tomorrow workers,
The citizens to keep it together and secure.
They are the pillars of the future.
I love you, Jersey.

A member of the Garden State

-25-

Walking into Forever

There is absolutely no doubt God is love and love comes from God. It is like the spice needed to bring life to the food. Nobody knows where love is. You cannot see it or touch it. It is like a mystery, but when it touches your heart, it changes you. It takes your breath away and often leaves you speechless.

Love also heals a broken heart. It brings people from different backgrounds together. It pushes people to help each other. If it were not for love, people would have already disappeared from the face of the earth. *Homo homini lupus*: they would kill each other.

Anne Marie apparently got back to normal, coming and going as usual, but deep inside, she had a kind of resentment that kept her away from people. She did not trust anymore. Mohammad was in the past, but the torments had left a scar that was constantly there to remind her of the old wounds. It would take love, patience, and understanding to bring back the confidence and the trust.

Benoit had been visiting, sending little notes. Sometimes he would call to check if she would like to go out or just to talk. Like a faithful servant, he was ready to run by her side anytime; but like a fine, fragile china, he was cautiously handling the situation. He was taking his time to show that he cared and got reacquainted with her. Like the time when they were in high school, every Friday afternoon, they would hang out in the charming and lively city of Hoboken. Together with Raquel, they would walk along Frank Sinatra Park eating ice cream. That was some time ago. Anne Marie kept everybody at a distance. Nevertheless, Benoit did not stop following her lead and did not care if he had to wait an eternity: "Love is patient."

When Méralie's husband passed away, he left her struggling with a handful: four children and lots of needs. It took her discipline, trust in God, and understanding to keep the family together. It was not easy, but love pushed her the extra miles.

She usually said, to love your fellow citizens, first you needed to love the land where you were born. As well, to love your neighbors, you needed to love your city, ready to support the activities going on in the community. With gratefulness for the country that had received her, Méralie's attachment for the community lay in the compassion and the love she had for her neighbors. As a mother, she had a soft spot for the youths—most of all, the ones going around without guidance.

"Tout pitit se pitit," she would say: the same way she loved her children, the next-door kids also deserved love.

She felt she had to do something to help; but no matter what she could do, her mission would be in Jersey City, the place she had been living since she left her homeland.

Love is a force. It moves us to take bold actions and do great things. It is a gift to humanity. It literally transcends people, nations, and religion. It is the universal language of this world, and people from different cultures and different backgrounds recognize it for what it is truly is. They understand the power that is in it.

Hellen and Hyppolite had never met before. They did not live in the same neighborhood or had the same acquaintances until, one day, a snowstorm brought them close to each other on the road. Soon they rapidly understood that love was as critical for the mind as oxygen for the body. Out of so many people crossing their paths every single day, the mystery of love chose them both, touching their hearts and souls; and they became indispensable for each other.

Two people, two souls from different walks of life, two hearts, and two lives merging as one. They decided to come forward and publicly declare before God and men they were in love. They wanted to join their souls together to say yes in a promise to never let go of each other.

The day of celebration finally came; Méralie could not be happier. Thanks to Raquel, who helped with the errands of the day, she was beautiful and ready before everybody. Anne Marie also was lovely; she was sparkling. Hyppolite spent the night at his mother's in preparation for the big day. Escorted by Tertulien, he was coming out of the room to go down to the limousine that was waiting for him. He stopped for a minute to hug his sister.

"This is your day, brother," said Anne Marie. "It's wonderful to see you happy. You deserve the best. May the blessing of God be on you and Hellen today and the rest of your lives."

"Thank you," said Hyppolite, who kept looking at her, perplexed.

Beyond the makeup, she had something special, radiant, not easy to tell that stood out from within. Was it her smile? Her eyes?

Touched by the transformation, Hyppolite could not help asking questions. "What is it? What causes this change? What is going on? Is it Benoit?"

Anne Marie wrapped her arms around her brother's shoulder and smiled. "I looked in the depth of his eyes," she said, "and something hit right in my heart. I suddenly felt peace and joy. He lifted my soul. It is like my life is waking up to a new day. For the first time, I feel someone is mine, and I am his. I think a bond is being formed between us, and it is a good feeling."

The wedding ceremony was as moving as it was beautiful. People from both sides abounded. Relatives who had watched them grow, classmates who had followed their trajectory in life, coworkers, and longtime neighbors gathered to share that special moment and congratulate the happy couple.

The officer delivered an eloquent message. "Marriage is a joyous occasion. It's connected in our thoughts with the charm of love, the warmth of a home. Getting married brings a lot of excitement and novelty into our life, but at the same time, it creates a new series of responsibilities and duties, requiring effort and commitment. It is a lifetime commitment, a promise between two people who love each other, who trust that love, who honor one another as individuals, and who wish to spend the rest of their lives together. But its sacredness and unity are the most significant covenant known in human relations. It enables the two separate souls to share their desires, longings, dreams, and memories, their joys and sorrows, and help each other through all uncertainty of life.

"Unlike family relationships or friendships, marriage is unique because it involves a conscious choice, a lifelong commitment, common goals, and very high compatibility. That is why, when a marriage is successful, it becomes more fulfilling than any other type of relationship.

"It is the bedrock of society. When two people are getting married, they want to create a home for their children, a place where they would grow and become healthy and successful citizens. May this be a beautiful beginning for a wonderful life."

In the recollection of a beautiful church on Kennedy Boulevard, Hellen and Hyppolite pledged their fidelity to one another—to love, honor, and cherish one another—and sealed it with a kiss in the presence of the lovely gathering that showered them with the best wishes.

The reception was held at Liberty House in Liberty State Park. Every eye was focused on the newlyweds. They spent their time thanking and acknowledging the presence of friends and family before they left. The party continued. People who had not seen each other for a long time were touching base, eating, and dancing. Raquel was sitting with Anne Marie and Benoit at the same table, listening to music and looking at the people.

"Life is strange," said Raquel. "From two perfect strangers, they become one happy couple. This is the miracle of love. I wish them the best."

"Love is born in our hearts in a very subtle way," commented Benoit. "It grows slowly until someone becomes indispensable. We are finally convinced that this is the right person, the one we want to share the rest of our lives with."

Raquel moved away from the table to chat with an old friend; Benoit finally asked for a dance. With the complicity of Raquel, as soon as they went to the floor, everybody moved back, leaving them in the middle. Soon a melody filled the air with the explosive and unmistakable voice of Dolly Parton:

> Take my hand and run with me
> Out of the past of yesterday
> And walk with me
> Into the future of tomorrow
> Yesterday must be forgot
> No looking back no matter what
> There's nothing there but
> Memories that bring sorrow
> Yesterday is gone, gone
> But tomorrow is forever

Suddenly Benoit dropped to his knees, holding a ring. "The love I have for you cannot be described even with the most romantic words. Ever since the day I met you, you have become the source of my inspiration. You are my love, my heart, my peace, and my joy. I love you beyond more than you can ever imagine. I will continue loving you until the end of time. I am asking you to marry me."

The surprise brought Anne Marie to tears. Shaking with emotion, she finally said yes in the middle of an ovation and cries of joy.

Méralie was speechless. When she got back to her senses, the first word that came out was "Beni soit l'Eternel" with her hands lifted.

-26-

The Tender Hearts

Meetings had become a habit in the family. When the children were young and one did something wrong, Méralie would deal with him separately. But mostly she would have regular meetings with everybody to express her discontent or to praise them.

Three weeks after the wedding, Hellen and Hyppolite received the rest of the family in their home in Secaucus. Everything was ready for a fun evening. Anne Marie came with Benoit; Méralie could not make it because of an emergency meeting in church. Sparkling of happiness, Hellen, this time, took the lead and wanted to say a few words.

"Hyppolite and I, we thank you all for being with us this evening. I have been thinking about this family, above all, Mamma Méralie, who always shows understanding and support in so many ways to other people. Like a bright light on a polished mirror, she reflects her love and wisdom on her family. She has succeeded in communicating the same affection to her children and keep them close to her heart. I am touched by the respect that binds you together. Now I understand why my husband is such a kind and loving man. I understand the sweet mystery hiding behind his gentleman kind and simplicity.

"Hyppolite, thank you for being my best friend. Thank you for being by my side. You are a blessing in my life. I am proud to be your wife. I pray we continue holding hand, looking in the same direction, cherishing every second, every minute that we live until the end. *Je t'aime!*"

"I love you too," said Hyppolite, hugging her and holding her hand. "I want to be your companion, your confidant, and your lover.

"I am happy to have you guys with me today," continued Hyppolite, addressing to his brothers. "I have been thinking about my trajectory from the day I came back to America. When I compare myself to the man you picked up some time ago at Gifford Avenue to bring home, my heart overflows with emotion. I have a lot to thank for.

"The fact is there are moments in life so scary and so frustrating that you would like to close your eyes and simply disappear forever. After the earthquake, I came to Jersey City with my heart in shambles. Every breath taken was a painful question to my existence. I was going through life wondering if God simply did not care. My constant grumpiness wasn't funny. But thanks to your patience and understanding, you were there for me. In my difficult times, you didn't let me down. I am sorry Mommy did not come today. She never stops talking faith into me, and thanks to her love and support, I survive the coup. For all these reasons, I thank God every day for bringing me to earth through this family.

"But still I had a sort of emptiness I couldn't explain. To no avail, I was looking for that alleviating light that would indicate the end of the tunnel and liberate me from my dark and profound misery. Like a starving dog, my soul, my heart, and my mind were in alert until the day, in the middle of a winter storm, Hellen, like an angel falling from heaven, crossed my path. I was so stubborn and badly hurt that I couldn't understand. I didn't want to hear about love, not even friendship.

"But Hellen came like the morning dew, resting upon my soul, mending my broken heart. Little by little, I learned to take one day at a time. I learned to get along with the wind, not to struggle with the flow, until the power of love set me free. I finally understand, no matter how hard you get beat up, no matter how tough the suffering is, there is always a seed of love left. Look deep enough. You will find it. Although the silence insists on cutting the words out of your mouth, the heart still take over, speaking through the eyes in the name of love."

The afternoon went by; everybody was having a good time. Hyppolite congratulated Anne Marie and Benoit on their engagement and offered his unconditional help.

"You are beautiful, little sister. It's obvious that you have changed. Your gaze, your demeanor says it all. Happiness shines in your smile. It is breathing through your pores. I feel a kind of calmness around you."

"The intense anguish and constant suspense that were oppressing my heart are now dwelling in the past," said Anne Marie, holding Benoit's hand. "Fear is no longer ruling my life."

After a moment of chatting, the conversation turned to a more important subject.

"We all seem to be moving on with our lives," said Tertulien. "I have been thinking about Mommy. We need to know what is going to happen with her. She is not getting younger."

"Mommy is okay," said Anne Marie. "She is very active in her church. Everybody seems to appreciate her in the community. I do not see any problem."

"That does not stop the years from passing by," replied Tertulien. "People live under the impression that we and our loved ones will never become old. I do not know where this idea comes from. Mommy is getting up in age. It is a reality that we cannot escape."

Since the conversation started, Esaie became nervous, scratching his head, walking back and forth, looking at his siblings, and moving around.

"What is it?" said Tertulien, who knew him better than anyone else. "What is going on?"

"Well," said Esaie, "I know we all have been thinking the same thing. Mommy cannot stay by herself in that house. I think it only makes sense that she moves with me when the time comes."

"What are you talking about?" responded Tertulien, gazing at them. "None of you can take care of Mom better than I do. Do you know her medications? Do you know the schedule needed for them? Do you know the store she does her grocery shopping? I need her as much she needs me."

"Listen!" intervened Anne Marie. "In case you did not notice, I am her only daughter. Mommy is staying with me. I am the best person to take care of her. I will get married soon and probably have children. She will be so happy to have babies around her. Hyppolite is attached to Mommy, and as much as I love him, he cannot have her with him. I feel like I am more stable as a woman. She will be better off with me."

The conversation was going nowhere; everybody had a good reason to have their mother at their side. They finally turned their gaze to Hellen and asked her opinion.

"Aging is a natural process," advised Hellen. "Sometimes it is painful to talk about, but it is always wise to be prepared because this a reality we must confront sooner or later. Méralie is a strong woman. So far, she does not show any sign of decline. It is true she is now older. At time, she complains of ache and pain, but that does not minimize the feeling of her heart or her passion for what she is doing."

"Mommy is not slowing down," said Anne Marie. "Her going around, speaking to the neighbors, has bear fruits. Her message got through. People start to understand the necessity to bend together to support the youths in their neighborhood. Now she has regular meetings every Saturday afternoon with some ladies. They form a group called the Tender Hearts. Some of them are ministers and retired professionals. They debate on the different problems going on. They discuss on how to approach parents on the subject, and they go back to their church, where they are mentoring different adolescent programs. Now Mommy is teaching ESL to a group of young immigrants just entering the country. She has won the respect and the appreciation of a lot of people."

"This is good," said Hellen. "Before you take any decision, I think you should speak to her and hear what she wants to do."

"Soon will be her birthday," said Hyppolite with the certainty that he was the preferred son of his mother. "While we celebrate with her, she will tell us exactly who she wants to live with."

-27-

Go in the Pursuit of Your Destiny

With Hellen at his side and backing him up, Hyppolite become an entrepreneur on a bigger scale. They just opened a rent-a-van and rent-a-truck business for local and residential movers. He put on hold his regular delivery job for a while to dedicate his time to this new project.

"So far, so good," said Hellen to a friend who was visiting the new place. "Hyppolite loves what he is doing. He is here every day, trying different approach to make it run better. He is a hard worker. His natural ability and dedication start to bear fruit. I am surprised beyond my expectation. We could have a bigger local, but he is a cautious man. He prefers going step-by-step. I am confident that soon the business will take another extension. His family is very supportive."

Anne Marie had been very busy putting her wedding plan together. With the help of her friend Raquel, they had also made necessary preparation for the party the family wanted to give Méralie for her birthday. That celebration was particularly important because everyone was planning to have their mother living with them. They were anxious to hear from her with whom she decided to go with.

"I have no doubt," said Anne Marie, "she will come to live with me. Mommy loves us all, and we love her too. Esaie has been talking about convincing her. He has put an extra bedroom in his new house, thinking, if he has more space, Mommy will be more comfortable. I do not say anything, but they ignore the bond between a mother and a daughter is something special. Let them get the surprise of their life."

In a luxurious and spacious venue at Liberty Park, the whole family gathered for that special occasion. The ambiance was friendly, and the music very welcoming. Esaie accompanied his inseparable fiancée, Yanique. They would soon tight the knot. Hyppolite did not move one step away from Hellen, whose stomach got bigger and bigger. The doctor said anytime now the baby would come. Benoit came in with his little brother, Harold, who became friends with Joseph.

Méralie, last, came in with Anne Marie and Tertulien. In the middle of an ovation, everybody raised their voice along with the music feeling the room.

Aujourd'hui c'est ta fête	Today is your day
Tu as mis ta robe de paillette	You have on your sequin dress
Tu es belle à voir.	You are so beautiful
Bon anniversaire	Happy birthday

"Today we get together to celebrate a hero," said Hyppolite. "Our mother is a warrior who had stood tall and strong in front of every adversity life has put her through. Being a widow too soon and at the cost of lots of sacrifices, she has raised her children without a man at her side. She has been a guide, an anchor for us. Even in our adult age, she never gives up on us. She never stops making sure we are all right.

"Mommy, we love you. We are lucky and proud to have you as our mother. You're a light, the sun that has been shinning throughout our life. You have built the morality stone we stand on. Regardless of the difficult times, you never lose faith. You never abandoned your goodness. Compassion and kindness are absolute in you. Mom, we love you because love is in your soul, love is in your heart, love is in your mind. Once again, happy, happy birthday! May you have many more birthdays with us."

Méralie looked all around; she was amazed by the elegance of the facility. The music, the song, and the ovation brought a teardrop of joy to her face. Moved by emotion, she took time before addressing to her audience.

"Thank so much for this celebration," she finally said. "You went in length and in large to make today a very special one. I don't have words to express how happy I am. I thank God for my family, and I thank you for the happiness you have brought me during all these years.

"I remember the first time I set foot in this country. I was lonely. I was scared. In Jersey City, where I settled, I did not have anyone to speak to. Most of all, I did not understand what people were telling me. Later, with my husband and my children, I wasn't alone anymore, but the fight for life wasn't easy.

"When I became a widow, the struggle was even more frightening, but every time I looked at my children smiling, running around the house, calling Mommy, I regained strength. Today I am looking at you, my heart rejoices. I cannot help blessing the Lord. My family is growing. I have my grandson, Joseph. Hyppolite's wife is about to give birth. I feel blessed. I know I will never be alone anymore. God is good. God is love. Love is so powerful that it heals. It restores. I thank you. May God bless you all."

The party was coming to an end. Anne Marie and Hellen were getting the flowers and the birthday cards together. Esaie, who was still nervous, brought the music down and approached his mother.

"Mommy, we have some concerns," he said. "We have been all together since we have been here, but everyone is getting married and moving on. You cannot stay alone in the house. I am sure Joseph will be living with his dad. So we would like to know which one of us you want to live with."

Immediately Anne Marie stood up, smiling as if she wanted to make herself noticed while Esaie and Tertulien looked at her, annoyed. Méralie instinctively felt the disagreement among them.

"It is a good thing that you all want me to live and stay with you," she said, gazing around and smiling. "But it is even better that you all know how to drive because I am not leaving my home."

Everybody looked at each other, shocked, and started speaking together.

"Mom, what are you saying?"

"But...but, Mommy!"

"Calm down," said Esaie. "You are stressing her out. Mom, what are you saying? It would be good if you move with one of us. Who would you prefer to stay with?"

"Absolutely not!" said Méralie. "At least not for the moment. I have been a mother for so many years. It will be hard to look around the house and see that it is nothing but an empty nest. It will be hard to redefine myself. I love my children dearly, but it would be selfish on my part to detain you in your course. Your freedom is my freedom. Your happiness, my happiness. Remember your joy. Your destiny is likely not going to come knocking at your door in the form of an omega jackpot check. You need to go for it! I have already lived my life. Now it is time for you to be emancipated. Spread your wings and soar like an eagle. I am getting old. I do not know what tomorrow will bring, but so far, so good. Like my own mother used to say, 'I will hang my bag where my hands can reach.' I promise you I will not push it beyond my strength. I will take it easy."

"You are not used to being alone," said Anne Marie. "We need to have you close and take care of you."

Staying quiet for a while, Méralie become pensive.

"I remember," she said, "I was a young girl, growing in a family where it was difficult to make ends meet. My mother was struggling beyond her strength to provide for us. As the firstborn, it was heartbreaking witnessing her pain and not able to do anything to help much. When I finally found the opportunity to move on, she did not want to let me go. 'It is not safe to leave your home, your family, with a group of strangers to a foreign country,' she said, and she was right. But I finally convinced her. She let me go in the pursuit of my destiny.

"I am happy to say that God did not abandon me. I have created my own family with four children. It was not easy. Your father was gone too soon. I struggled a lot, but thank God, you are where you are today. Like a mother hen, I kept you under my wings, watching you grow, trying to raise you with discipline and respect. And even you grew past eighteen, I kept you close to my heart.

"Today I am telling you the same thing I said thirty years ago, 'Go in the pursuit of your destiny.' Remember, the road to a dream is not easy to navigate. Life has its ups and downs, often dotted with mountains to climb, obstacles to overcome, and hard, mind-numbing times that make you feel like quitting. Be flexible, patient, and courageous. Sometimes you will have to bend to let the storm pass over. In case you get lost along the way, remember, anything that is worth having does not come easy. Do not turn around. Do not give up. Keep pressing forward. Believe in God. Have faith in your abilities. Where there is a will, there is a way. Keep your hands clean from any wrongdoing, but never give up.

"Hyppolite got married. They will most likely continue living in Secaucus. Esaie has a property in Connecticut. He is about to get married. Tertulien's wife has an appointment at the American embassy in Port-au-Prince. I am sure he will follow her to Brooklyn, where she has relatives. They even have a job offer waiting for her.

"Benoit loves Anne Marie. This young man, I do not know what to tell him. He has already introduced his family to our family. Now Anne Marie has accepted him. I am sure they will not take long. I praise the Lord every day for his grace and mercy."

"Mommy," said Esaie, "we love you dearly. We will never be able to repay you for all your sacrifices. All this time you have been in New Jersey, you never had a chance to visit any other place. You could not afford any vacation because of us. We know you are not too interested in traveling by boat or airplane. But if you are with us, we will be able to take you out every now and then. At least, spend the weekend, like the last time. There are so many beautiful and peaceful resorts in New Jersey."

"Visiting New Jersey is wonderful!" said Méralie, smiling. "I will never forget the beautiful place you took me last time for the weekend. It is paradise on earth. I do not have to leave my place and move somewhere else. Now you are about to have your own family, do not worry too much.

"The Good Word said, 'A man will leave his father and mother and be united to his wife, and the two will become one flesh. So they are no longer two but one flesh.'

"Therefore, my job is done! I am not moving anywhere. I like it here. I am familiar with almost everybody in the neighborhood.

Some of the ladies and I, we have a job to do counseling, advising, preaching anyone who wants to listen. My greatest satisfaction is Albert, who is a new person now. He found himself a job. He is straightening out. He goes to church. It is a grace."

"It is nice you are doing some activities, trying to help in the community," said Esaie. "But you are not getting younger. You need to relax and enjoy things you couldn't have before."

"My gray hair, my wrinkles, my aches, and pains tell only a part of my story, which is the constant struggle with the inexorable time passing by. But there are things I cannot explain, things that you don't study in a classroom or read in a book. You need to be in the school of life to understand them. I can tell you, though, every wrinkle of my face is a mark of wisdom that forces me to neither judge nor hold kindness to anyone coming my way. It is a joy and a satisfaction to lend a hand to someone who need help.

"I have been living so long in this neighborhood I do not see myself jumping from one place to another. My church is not too far from here. The store, the supermarket, they are within walking distance. Changing address would be like deprograming myself and starting new. You cannot teach old dog new tricks."

"But, Mommy!" yelled everyone.

"Now you are all grown. You need to continue your way. Follow your dream. Keep up the good work for your own sake, for the sake of your family and your community. Life has never been easy. If you are breathing under the sun, the struggle continues. My doors will be always open for you and your family. But I do not want to depart from Garden State, the Jersey of my love!"

Garden State

God blessed Garden State with the exceptional!
Its regions are incredibly beautiful and natural!
The Skylands' rolling hills and mountains astonish
Crystal-clear lakes and mighty rivers refresh
From the great wildlife refuge of the wetlands
To the national parks, the beauty outstands
Going to Cumberland County by Delaware Bay
All is pleasure; for a nice vacation, it is the best way
The Pinelands has a narrow, twisting stream
Flowing through oak and cedar like a dream
The windy fringe of shoreline stretching to Cape May
The canoeist's marvel, paradise every day
Enjoy the natural wonders of the Jersey Shore
Wildwood and Great Adventure leave you craving more
At the Gateway Region stands tall Lady Liberty
Giving passes to adventure, freedom, and beauty
Garden State, with its bountiful fruits and vegetables
Is like a diamond in the sunshine: it sparkles
As a melting pot of race, culture, and colors
History writes herself with golden letters
When enjoying great outdoors and exotic flowers
You will find out there a lot more wonders
Yet a great deal of excitement left still to discover
New Jersey will steal your very soul over and over

About the Author

Exileine was born in Jérémie, a city in the Grand'Anse Department in Haiti.

Exileine completed high school in Port-au-Prince, the capital, where she attended college and majored in social work. After her arrival in the United States, she entered New Jersey University, where she completed her studies in sociology. Including English and Creole, she also speaks three other languages.

When Exileine is not writing, she is an avid lover of music and enjoys gardening and spending time with her family, including her grandchildren.

Being a native for over thirty years, Exileine has such a deep love and gratitude for the Garden State.

Her love of nature and romance and attention to detail bring her characters to life and make her an exquisite storyteller.